MOON MAGIC

MOON MAGIC

LUNAR SPELLS TO ATTRACT AN ENCHANTED LIFE

MARIE BRUCE

SIRIUS

All images courtesy of Shutterstock

This edition published in 2024 by Sirius Publishing, a division of
Arcturus Publishing Limited,
26/27 Bickels Yard, 151–153 Bermondsey Street,
London SE1 3HA

ISBN: 978-1-3988-4491-9
AD011388UK

Printed in China

Dedicated to my brother, Ian, who presented me with my first electric typewriter back in 1994 and told me to get on with it. I've been a published author ever since.

And for all those who like to worship the moon goddess. Blessed be.

CONTENTS

INTRODUCTION

PER ARDUA AD ASTRA

Through Adversity to the Stars

Welcome to the world of moon magic, where the night sky shines bright with possibility and shooting stars herald the arrival of new opportunities. Witches have always worked with the power of the moon. We use its pull to manifest our goals and to draw positive things into our lives. Working with lunar energy is an intrinsic part of spell casting and pagan rituals.

The night sky is full of mystery and magic, beauty and magnificence. To be spellbound, all you have to do is look up and gaze at the stars or the orb of the full moon. *Per ardua ad astra* is a Latin phrase which loosely translates to mean *through adversity to the stars,* and while this phrase is perhaps best known for being the motto of the British Royal Air Force, it can also be a good mantra for anyone who wishes to improve their life using the magic of the moon and stars.

Life can be difficult at times and everyone is going through something, but with magic at your fingertips you can take steps to minimize the negative events and maximize the positive outcomes in your life. In this book you will learn how to set up a magical moon altar, how to tap into the power of the lunar cycle, and how to use moon magic to manifest your goals. In addition, you will find meditations, rituals, totem animals and dream-weaving spells, allowing you to make the very most of the night sky and the power of the moon goddess, each and every night

of your life. It's time to embrace the moon-cast shadows and tap into your nocturnal power, with the enchanting practice of Moon Magic.

This is a world where sweet dreams come true!

Serene blessings,
Marie Bruce x

CHAPTER ONE
WITCHES MOON

There are few more beautiful sights than that of a full moon on a clear night. The moon is the most recognizable part of our universe and one that even the smallest child can identify. Other planets may remain a mystery, but the moon is our close companion. She watches over us as we sleep, she lights the sky at night, beaming her silvery glow over the world, creating an enchanted landscape. She provides vital illumination for soldiers on night missions and casts a romantic glow over lovers in the gloaming, sharing their first kiss. She is a gentle, yet powerful presence, pulling at the tides with her magnetic force, waxing and waning as she moves in orbit around the earth.

The moon and magic go hand in hand. Images of witches dancing naked under the full moon were often used as propaganda during the witch hunts of the past and even today, we are bombarded with pictures of witches flying across the moon on broomsticks, every October in the run-up to Halloween. While broomstick flight might be no more than the flight of fancy, there is some truth in the naked dancing, for covens of witches sometimes like to work naked, or skyclad as it is also known, when celebrating seasonal changes. This lack of clothing denotes the freedom of birth and the natural state, but it is by no means compulsory. You can perform moon magic just as effectively while remaining fully dressed, and on a dark winter night, warm clothing is certainly advised!

WITCHES AND THE MOON

Witches have a very special relationship with the moon. While we do not *worship* her as such, we do cast our spells in accordance with the lunar cycle, each phase being used for a particular type of magic. We hold special rituals, called Esbats, to mark the new and full lunar phases each month. We see the moon as being representative of the divine feminine, hence why we refer to her with feminine pronouns. She is known as the Lady or the Goddess and she is a vital force of magic that witches tap into when casting spells or performing rituals.

Rarely does a witch cast a spell without first consulting a lunar calendar to see where the moon is in her cycle. We cast magic in her light, drawing on her power to magnetize the things we dream of and bring them into being. If the earth is our mother, then the moon is our grandmother. We connect with her through the constant changes of the lunar cycle, pulling things towards us as she waxes to full, then releasing the things that no longer serve us as she wanes away to dark moon. In this way, we are always connected to her lunar energies.

CREATE A LUNAR ALTAR

Setting up a lunar altar in your home is a great way to connect with the moon's power. Having a special place dedicated to the moon and your magical practice is one of the ways you can begin to invite the magical light of the moon into your life.

Begin by collecting items which depict or represent the moon, so postcards, pictures, ornaments, candle holders, crystals, mirrors and so on. Find a place in your home to use as a moon altar. This could be a windowsill, a countertop or a small side table. You might like to cover it with a white or silver cloth, but this is optional. Next arrange all your items in a pleasing way, ensuring that you have a couple of candles ready to burn, placed towards the back of the altar. Add an incense burner and your altar is ready for magical use.

You can use this space to cast spells, perform rituals, lay out divination card spreads and to light incense in honour of any lunar deities you are working with. Add a statue of the lunar totem animals you connect with too and make this a space that is personal to you and your magical moon journey. Finally, bless the space by sprinkling a little spring water over the altar and saying the following words.

I dedicate this sacred space to the lunar light of the moon's magical grace.

THE LUNAR CYCLE

In order to cast with the power of the moon, you first need to understand her cycle and how she works. The moon takes around 27 days to complete one full orbit around the earth. It also takes approximately 29 days to go from one new moon to the next – this is called a lunar month. Already, you can see the parallels between the lunar cycle and the female menstrual cycle. This is another one of the reasons why the moon is referred to in the feminine. Magically speaking, each point in the lunar cycle represents an aspect of spell-casting, which are as follows.

New Moon

This is the beginning of the lunar cycle, although the moon cannot actually be seen in the sky until a few days after the new moon. For this reason, the start of the new moon phase is sometimes known as dark moon and is typically a time of rest. As soon as the first sliver of light appears, however, it is time to start thinking about what you want the next lunar cycle to bring you. The new moon is a time for sowing the seeds of new projects, weighing up the pros and cons of a situation, assessing the need for a change in your patterns etc. Remember that all seeds are sown in darkness, to grow with the light. Now is the time to decide what you want.

Waxing Crescent

The light increases from the right, showing a crescent moon that looks like a backwards C shape. This is the time when you set your intention – set your mind on exactly what it is you want. You don't need to know how you will achieve the goal, just set your intention and allow the universe to work out the details for you.

First Quarter Moon

In this phase the moon looks like it has been cut in half – half of it is illuminated by the sun, the other half remains in darkness. Now is the time to take action on your intentions, so brush up your CV or start applying for jobs if a career change is your goal. Make a positive start on a new project. Get out more and meet new people if you want to draw new friends to you. Make a start on your goal, even if only in a small way.

Waxing Gibbous

The moon now appears to be three quarters full, with most of it brightening our night sky. Now is the time to start walking your talk. It's not enough to have a goal, you need to take consistent action and work towards it. The lunar energies won't do the work for you! It is a collaboration and you need to put the effort in too. At this time, the energies are growing stronger and magnetically pulling in your intention, so help it along with positive action.

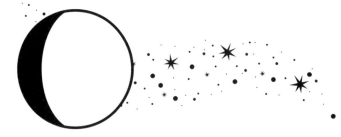

Full Moon

The full moon lights up the night sky and her effect can be felt by everyone, all over the world. This is a time of abundance, of goals coming to fruition and labouring on long-term ambitions. The full moon offers a boost of energy if you are flagging in your aspirations, lending much-needed energy to your goal. The energy of the full moon can be felt for three nights in a row – the night before, the night of, and the night after the moon is full. This is also the most powerful time for all kinds of magic, divination and spell casting, so don't waste it!

Waning Gibbous

As the moon begins to wane, now is the time to show gratitude for what this lunar cycle has brought you so far. Reflect on what worked and what projects are still in progress. Big ambitions take more than one lunar cycle to manifest, so use this time to assess where you are on the path to achievement and reflect on what your next steps should be. Think about what has worked well for you and what you would like to change or do better at in the next lunar cycle.

Last/Third Quarter Moon

This is the time to start releasing anything that no longer serves you. Let go of old grudges, bad relationships, mistakes made, toxic habits and so on. In this phase, the moon requires you to be honest with yourself, to identify the toxic behaviours and bad habits that might be contributing to a negative situation, so that you can release those too.

Waning Crescent/Balsamic Moon

This phase marks the end of the lunar cycle, when the moon shows up in the sky as the classic fairy-tale c-shaped crescent. It is a time to reflect and move deeper into self-awareness. This is a good time to cast banishing spells as the moon's energy helps to pull things away from you. Slowly the light will fade out, night by night, until we are back at the dark moon and the cycle begins once more, so it is never too late for a fresh start and each moon cycle offers a new opportunity to begin again.

As you attune more with the phases of the moon you will come to understand how it affects you personally. You might find that you are full of beans and ideas shortly after the new moon, but your enthusiasm wanes after the full moon. Many people report experiencing vivid dreams during the full moon. Keep a note of any special experiences you have and where the moon was in her cycle at the time. Be aware that the moon is in the same phase all over the world. Remember that the moon's energies can still be felt by day too. She is always there, influencing us from above, even though we can't always see her bright orb in the sky. Her power is constant, though her appearance is ever changing.

ADMIRATION FOR THE MOON

Most witches tend to perform rituals to honour the moon and acknowledge the power she holds over the earth. It is how we connect with her magnetic force. It is a way of checking in with her as a force of nature. Witches always refer to the moon using the feminine pronoun, because we see her as being the embodiment of the Great Goddess. In attuning with the lunar cycle, we are connecting to the divine feminine and bringing her energies into our lives in a more intentional way. There are lots of ideas throughout this book for ways in which you can honour the moon, so there should be no reason why you cannot start your moon magic practice right away, regardless of which phase the moon is currently in. Let's begin with a simple visualization.

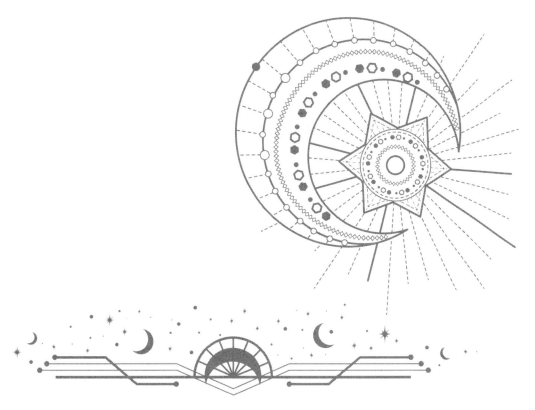

MOON VISUALIZATION

This visualization is great for when you feel that you want a boost of lunar energy, but you cannot see the moon in the sky for whatever reason. Sit in a quiet place and plant your feet firmly on the floor so that your own energy remains grounded. Close your eyes and breathe deeply a few times, until you feel nice and relaxed. Now picture yourself sitting on a beautiful beach as dusk falls. You can hear the sound of the waves gently lapping into shore. Imagine

yourself gazing out to sea and watch as a brilliant full moon slowly begins to rise up on the horizon. See the light becoming brighter, casting a silvery moonlit path along the ocean between the moon and where you sit upon the shore. Silently ask the moon goddess for her blessings and breathe in her light. Imagine her silver beams filling your lungs and healing every part of you that might be out of kilter. When you feel ready, thank the moon goddess for her energies, open your eyes and go about your day.

SET YOUR INTENTION FOR THE LUNAR MONTH

One of the main reasons why witches tend to get ahead in life is because we practise intentional living. By this I mean that we make a habit of setting our intention to accomplish something and then we take the necessary steps to achieve it. When you do this on repeat, you tend to start seeing results quite quickly, especially if you add a specific timeframe to the intention.

Using the lunar cycle as a timeframe is a great way to make sure that you remain on track with your intentions. You can set a different intention for each moon cycle of the year, working with the energies of the seasons as well as the lunar energies. For instance, you could set an intention on the new moon of January to work on your finances or your love life. As the moon waxes toward full, you would take steps to generate new income streams, save money or meet new people and go on more dates. Then as the moon begins to wane, you would use those diminishing energies to pull away anything that is standing in the way of your financial or romantic happiness, such as old debts, bad spending habits, lingering resentment for an ex-partner and so on. In this way, you are using the energies of the lunar cycle to help you achieve your goal. You can then reaffirm the intention on the next new moon, or if you have already achieved the goal, set a new intention to work on instead.

SPELL TO SET A LUNAR INTENTION

You will need:

a pen

a piece of paper

a piece of white ribbon

On the night of the new moon, take these items to your lunar altar and light the candles there to illuminate the space. Light some incense too if you want to. Now think about what you want to achieve in the next 29 days. Is there something that you have always wanted to try, or achieve? It could be that you are considering taking up a new sport, joining a drama class or going off to university. Whatever it is, write down your goal on the sheet of paper in the following way;

Throughout the moon of this month, my intention is to (name your goal) and these are the steps I will take to complete this task: (list the steps you will need to take to achieve your goal)

Next roll the piece of paper into a scroll and tie it with the ribbon. Leave the scroll on your lunar altar for the full lunar cycle. Try to make sure that your intentions are things that can be completed in the space of a month, or if they are bigger goals such as going to university, then break the overall goal down into smaller steps that can be completed over several months, with each month having three to four tasks for you to complete, as you work toward the bigger goal. Once you have completed all the tasks for your lunar

intention, then burn the scroll at the end of the lunar cycle, during a dark moon and set a new intention on the next new moon. In this way you are using the power of the moon to keep your life moving forward.

HOW TO MAKE MOON OIL

Spells and rituals sometimes call for special oils to be used, perhaps to anoint a candle or to dab onto a charm or talisman of some kind. This special lunar oil is a good all-purpose spell oil that you can use for a variety of spell-castings and because it is attuned to the moon, it can amplify the power of candle burning rituals, magical baths and so on.

You will need to make this lunar oil on the night before the full moon. Take a small 20-30ml jar and fill it with sweet almond oil. Then add five drops each of the following essential oils, jasmine, ylang ylang and sandalwood, followed by a half a teaspoon of vanilla essence. Put the lid on the jar and shake it to mix the oils together, then set the jar on a windowsill where it can soak up the light of the full moon. Leave it to charge in the moonbeams for three nights. It is then ready to use in your magic spells and rituals.

GARDENING AND THE MOON

Green-fingered witches have long understood the benefits of gardening in tune with the lunar cycle. This is because the gravitational pull of the moon also has an impact on how well plants grow. In fact, gardening in alignment with the different moon phases can help your garden and house plants to thrive and flourish. Most witches agree that herbs planted during a waxing moon tend to do better than those planted during a waning moon. Bear the lunar cycle in mind if you are keen on green witchery. Try to perform your gardening tasks in accordance with the phases of the moon, using these simple guidelines to help you.

Dark Moon – Usually considered to be a time of rest, just before the new moon appears in the night sky. Neither magic nor gardening is done during this phase, but you could use this phase to read gardening magazines, dream up ideas for new flower beds, catalogue your seeds or write about the benefits of certain plants in your Book of Shadows.

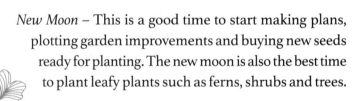

New Moon – This is a good time to start making plans, plotting garden improvements and buying new seeds ready for planting. The new moon is also the best time to plant leafy plants such as ferns, shrubs and trees.

Waxing Moon – As the moon grows from new to full, this is the time to plant seeds, move seedlings outdoors and put your garden plans into action. This is also the correct lunar phase to plant anything that bears fruit or berries.

Full Moon – As the moon reaches her peak and greatest power, now is the time to start replanting anything that needs more space, so start to repot and move plants to larger pots and beds. This is a good time to harvest fruit, berries and especially magical herbs, or for cutting flowers for the house.

Waning Moon – As the moon begins to wane and the light diminishes, this is the right time to tend to the darker aspects of the garden and anything which prefers darkness such as root crops and tubers. Tend to the soil, feed the root systems of trees and shrubs, and plant new bulbs that you want to grow in the spring such as bluebells and daffodils. The waning moon should also be the time for deadheading, pruning, cutting back and lopping trees.

IN THE NIGHT GARDEN

If you are a keen gardener and you have the space, why not consider creating a moon garden? These are gardens that are entirely made up of white flowers and silvery foliage and they are specifically designed to look most beautiful by moonlight. If you don't have a garden why not create a smaller moon garden by filling pots or window boxes with white flowering plants such as jasmine, camomile and daisy? Moon gardens have an ethereal, almost ghostly atmosphere, as the white flower heads nod in the night breeze and the silver-hued foliage shimmers in the moonbeams. Often, such flowerbeds are round or crescent in shape, to further reflect the beauty of the moon and they might include decorative silver orbs, water features, fountains and round mirrors. Anything that reflects the moonlight, such as crystals and glass wind-chimes, even a moon dial, can be incorporated into a moon garden. Try to plant flowers that bloom at twilight such as moonflower, jasmine and night scented phlox, or which have a pleasant scent such as white roses, peonies, hydrangeas and night scented violet. Add in a few herbs that are used for sleep remedies and dreaming rituals such as camomile and mugwort, and you are well on your way to an enchanting night garden. This garden will be a special place where you can come to meditate on warm summer evenings, or to enjoy a cup of hot cocoa in winter as you listen out for the hoot of an owl enjoying a moonlit night.

CHAPTER TWO
MOONLORE

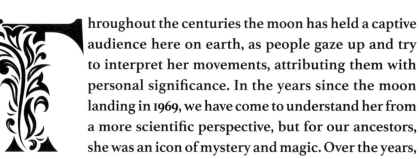

hroughout the centuries the moon has held a captive audience here on earth, as people gaze up and try to interpret her movements, attributing them with personal significance. In the years since the moon landing in 1969, we have come to understand her from a more scientific perspective, but for our ancestors, she was an icon of mystery and magic. Over the years, many superstitions evolved, from paying tribute to the moon to ward away bad luck, to using her cycle as a way of keeping time, in the days before the calendar was invented. In this chapter we will look at some of the popular folklore that has been influenced by the mystery of the moon.

NAME THAT MOON

Long before the calendar we know today was invented, people used the moon as a way of keeping track of time and marking the passing seasons. They did this by giving each full moon a special name. In this way they tracked the cycle of the seasons, each month having a moon which was named for the seasonal changes of that time of the year. Even the word *month* is derived from the word moon, so each year was divided into moons or months. Some of these lunar names are still in use today. We might talk of the Harvest Moon or the Wolf Moon, for instance. Although there are slight variations in the names for each moon from region to region, two naming systems have stood the test of time; the traditional country names and the

shamanic names from some Native American cultures. In naming each full moon, it became a reflection of what was happening on the earth during that time, as you will see from the examples below.

Traditional Country Moons

January – Wolf Moon

February – Storm or Ice Moon

March – Chaste, Worm or Death (of winter) Moon

April – Seed or Growing Moon

May – Hare or Flower Moon

June – Dryad or Strawberry Moon

July – Mead or Buck Moon

August – Wyrt or Barley Moon

September – Harvest or Corn Moon

October – Hunter's or Blood Moon

November – Snow or Beaver Moon

December – Oak, Cold or Winter's Moon

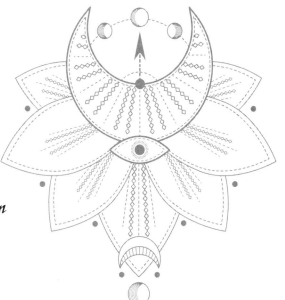

Shamanic Moons

Although the actual dates vary for the shamanic moons, usually beginning on the 10th or 11th of the month, they can roughly be divided like so:

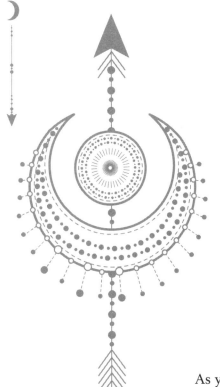

January ~ Deep Snows Moon

February ~ Strong Winds Moon

March ~ Fast Water-flow Moon

April ~ Planting Moon

May ~ Flowering Moon

June ~ Drying Up Moon

July ~ Hot Winds Moon

August ~ Hunter's Moon

September ~ Ripening Moon

October ~ Harvest Moon

November ~ Popping Trees Moon

December ~ Hard Freeze Moon

As you can see, the same seasonal themes occur within both traditions, so there are moons for harvest, hunters, snow, ice and the new growth of spring. In this way the moon acted as a vital prompt, reminding people when to plant, when to bring in the crops, when

to slaughter livestock or hunt for meat and when to retreat indoors as the winter weather closed in.

The moon was a visual cue for the agricultural year and the tasks required to ensure survival. Only a fool would leave livestock in the fields during the Wolf Moon, when the wolves of old would come closer to villages in search of food. Instead, animals would be brought into barns and shelters closer to the homestead, where they could be watched over more easily, safe from the hungry pack. While we no longer have to worry about wolves roaming through our gardens and snacking on the pet rabbit, it is still beneficial to learn these old names for the full moon of each month because it reinforces our link with the land and connects us to our ancestors. This is the lunar calendar which they would have lived by.

ATTUNING WITH THE MOON

Try to spend a little time each evening attuning with the energies of the moon. Go outside and bathe in her light. Breathe it in. Learn to recognize what phase she is in simply by looking at the night sky. This might take some time, but practice makes perfect. Feel how the energy changes as the moon goes through the various stages of her cycle. Once you have been doing this for several months, begin to test yourself by trying to guess the lunar phase when you are indoors, without looking through the window or using your phone! Can you pick up on the lunar energies? Can you *feel* what phase the moon is in? Attuning with the moon in this way can help to sharpen your instincts and hone your skills of perception. Bear

in mind that we are instinctively drawn to her power and spending time beneath the moonlight is as natural as sunbathing on a hot day. Try not to get spooked by the wildlife who are more active during the darker hours and make sure that you are in a safe space, such as your garden.

LUNAR SUPERSTITIONS

A superstition is the common belief that something has a supernatural power to bring about either good or bad luck. In the past, the world was a naturally much more superstitious place, because we didn't have a lot of science to make sense of our environment. Failed crops, plagues, pandemics and destructive weather patterns were often regarded as signs of witchcraft or demonic interference.

To counteract these ill favours, people came up with common practices that were thought to keep such bad luck at bay. These practices might involve carrying a charm to attract good luck or to ward away evil, or never stepping into the shadow of a suspected witch, for instance.

Fear of the unknown, ignorance, and events which couldn't be explained in a pre-scientific era led people to develop their own forms of comfort and the common superstition was born. Many of these superstitious practices became so well known that some people still adhere to them today, without even thinking about it. For example, when was the last time you walked under a ladder? You probably didn't. You probably walked around it, because superstition states that to walk beneath a ladder is bad luck!

Unsurprisingly, the moon has attracted quite a few superstitions of her own, ranging from the belief that the full moon causes madness to the more benevolent trope that lovers who first kiss beneath a full moon are blessed. Let's take a look at a few more lunar superstitions.

☾ It is unlucky to see a new moon through a window. If this happens you should open the window and invite the lunar light into your home as an honoured guest.

☾ The time of the full moon is said to bring about prophetic dreams, especially if you sleep in the moon's rays, while the dreams you have during the waning or dark moon tend to

highlight your fears and concerns and are more likely to turn into nightmares.

☾ It is said to be unlucky to point directly at the moon, but blowing her a kiss will bring good fortune your way.

☾ Seeing the full moon swathed in mist is a sign of trouble to come, which can be alleviated by saying "*Mother Moon in the mist, blink clear your eye and send no sorrow to my loved ones and I*".

☾ Seeing a halo around a full moon indicates a sharp frost and a colder turn in the weather.

☾ The full moon of March is sometimes known as the Death Moon because it represents the death of winter.

☾ Spotting the moon over your shoulder is bad luck. You should turn around and face the moon directly, giving her a nod, to turn the bad luck away.

☾ A full moon on a Monday is extremely auspicious and heralds a month of good fortune, while a full moon on a Sunday heralds the opposite.

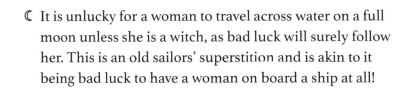

❨ It is unlucky for a woman to travel across water on a full moon unless she is a witch, as bad luck will surely follow her. This is an old sailors' superstition and is akin to it being bad luck to have a woman on board a ship at all!

❨ To see the black disk of a dark moon means that a storm is coming.

❨ Turning your coins over in the light of a new moon brings prosperity for the rest of the month.

❨ Never pay your bills during a waning moon or the money will not return to you. Pay them during a waxing moon and the cash will return threefold.

❨ Always cut your hair during a waxing moon to ensure it grows back thick and healthy.

❨ Brushing your hair in moonlight is said to enhance your allure.

❨ Seeing the moon reflected in a body of water such as a lake, loch or the sea is a sign of emotional upheaval to come.

❨ To see a red moon is a sign of bad luck.

BOWING TO THE MOON

In many magical traditions and esoteric practices, it is customary to make some kind of courtly bow to the moon. From the lunar salutations of yoga, to the Wiccan practice of an Esbat ritual, acknowledging the moon in some way is thought to be a beneficial practice and it is also said to bring about good fortune. Typically, a bow would be made at both the new and full moon, but you can acknowledge her light every night if you wish. Bowing to the moon is a traditional practice in some Eastern religions, while in the West it was more common to give a nod. Whatever way you decide to make your courtly bow, the important thing is that you acknowledge the moon in some way, particularly when she is new and also at her fullest, so just pretend you've dropped something and bow down in her light – no-one else need ever know that you have just offered a salutation to the moon!

MOON MADNESS

The notion that the moon can contribute to crazy behaviour has been in play for a long time. Perhaps it is no more than an urban myth, but many professional people, be they vets, midwives or police officers, claim that a full moon marks a much busier time.

It is commonly believed that a full moon has such a powerful influence on human behaviour that there are more accidents, more crimes and random acts of violence committed, more births and emergencies etc. during the time of the full moon, but this idea has

never been scientifically proven. It could simply be that the bright light of a full moon leads to more people being out and about much later into the evening, resulting in a corresponding spike in incidents, but it certainly makes you wonder doesn't it?

For centuries the moon has been thought to cause madness, hence the word *lunatic*, which of course derives from the word *lunar*, from which we get the modern terminology of lunacy, loony or loon, all used to denote someone of questionable sanity. Then of course there is the werewolf legend, where people are said to turn into crazy monsters around the time of the full moon!

It can be difficult to separate fact from fiction when it comes to the moon's influence on human behaviour, but it would be crazy not to even consider it as a possibility. The moon has an effect on the ocean tides and many people garden and plant crops at certain points of the lunar phase to make the most of these magnetic lunar energies, so why wouldn't the moon have an effect on mental health too? Much more research needs to be done before we can say one way or the other, but until it is a categorically disproven theory, people all over the world will still believe that the full moon makes some individuals behave in very odd ways!

BLOOD ON THE MOON

Witches often talk about there being *blood on the moon* which is when the moon has a rusty reddish glow. This term is not to be confused with the full moon of October, also known as the Blood Moon and which was traditionally the time when animals were slaughtered and the meat preserved for the winter months. The term *blood on the moon* can refer to any moon of the year and means that a time of misfortune, bad luck and upheaval is coming. It happens during a total lunar eclipse, when the sun's light is refracted through the earth's shadow, thus casting an eerie red glow upon the moon. This occurs approximately every eighteen months to two years.

In a magical sense, witches often use this special moon to process negative thoughts and emotions, or to come to terms with a difficult loss of some kind. It is a time for shadow work and deep psychological healing, which isn't always easy, but which is usually beneficial in the long term. When there is blood on the moon you can expect tempers to flare, tears to fall, and occasionally, blood to spill as people tend to become more accident prone when they are in a heightened emotional state. Perhaps this is the reason why this moon has a bad reputation for bringing conflict. Suffice to say that when there is blood on the moon, trouble isn't usually that far behind!

Spiritually, a lunar eclipse is generally a good time to evaluate your relationships, both personal and professional, and it can be the herald of big changes to come, so seeing *blood on the moon* could be an indication that a whole new path is about to be presented to you, leading you in a completely different direction. This shift in energies can be stressful at times, but this is an opportunity for a new beginning and a fresh start. In some ways, the *blood on the moon* is symbolic of the blood of childbirth and indicates that a rebirth of some kind is on the cards, but this will usually follow on from a time of emotional turmoil and upheaval.

BLOOD ON THE MOON SPELL

You can use this spell to alleviate the negative impact of a full lunar eclipse. This is a preventative spell, so do not wait until you see blood on the moon to cast it. Instead, use a lunar calendar to look up when the next total lunar eclipse will be and cast this spell the week before that full moon. Take a small red candle and anoint it with lunar oil (see page 27). As you rub the oil onto the candle visualize a time of peace and harmony for you and your family. Imagine the light from this candle casting a cloak of protection over you, keeping any trouble at bay and ensuring that the blood on the moon has no ill effects on you and your loved ones. Place the candle in a holder, light it and say:

Blood on the moon, I ask this boon
May you pass by me and mine, in goodness may you shine
No trouble for any here, for soon your light shines clear
In peace and harmony, so mote it be.

Let the candle burn down naturally, bringing peace of mind as it burns.

THE BEAUTY OF THE MOON

Just as the moon is a beautiful satellite, so too was it said to enhance the allure of those who performed beauty rituals in moonlight. Lots of old-fashioned beauty spells and rituals from the past were meant to be cast in the light of the full moon. This was a type of traditional folk magic, practiced by the common people and used to give a sense of personal agency over their lives. In the past, many a young maiden would have gathered moon dew for her beauty spells, to enhance her powers of attraction. Here then are a selection of rituals to help you harness the beauty of the moon.

Lunar Hair Care

Having long luscious locks of hair is the dream of many and this can be achieved more easily if you align your hair care in accordance with the moon. In fact, some salons even offer what is known as a *full moon cut,* which is basically your normal hair cut with a few esoteric extras thrown in, such as a soothing scalp massage using a hair oil, crystal therapy, detangling using a crystal comb, Reiki and so on. But you don't need to pay for an expensive salon treatment, as you can incorporate full moon treatments into your hair care routine at home.

Traditionally the best time to cut hair is just before the full moon, rather than on the full moon itself. This is said to encourage regrowth, resulting in longer, thicker hair. Cutting hair on a waning moon is thought to increase hair loss, so it is best avoided. Using oils to massage the scalp stimulates the follicles and encourages

hair to grow, or you could invest in a special hair massager and use that as you shampoo your hair.

In the Far East, women have long used rice water to maintain the gloss and bounce of their locks. Rice water is full of vitamins which help to strengthen hair and can stimulate growth, while the starch coats the hair, meaning that it also works well as a detangling solution. You can make your own rice water by simply boiling some rice and straining the water to use as a hair mist, or you can invest in one of the many rice water hair care products that are available, for greater convenience. Interestingly, rice is commonly known as one of the moon grains, which along with oats and barley, are

said to increase strength and stamina, so it would be an ideal addition to any lunar hair care routine, especially if you leave the rice water in the light of the full moon before using it, to soak up the lunar energies.

Full Moon Brushing Charm

A traditional beauty ritual from the past was to go outside and brush your hair by the light of the moon. This was said to add a luminous shine to your locks, and as mentioned earlier, it was thought to enhance your allure. The night of the full moon was the most auspicious time to do this, so why not give it a try? When the full moon has fully risen in the sky, take your hair brush and find a spot to sit in the moonlight. Then slowly brush out your hair and as you do so, say the following brushing charm. You can enhance the spell by using a silver-backed hairbrush or a silver comb, as silver is linked to the moon.

Luscious locks that gleam and shine
Enchanted be this hair of mine
By light of moon and silver beams
My hair now grows is shining reams!

GATHERING MOON DEW

In the hours just before dawn when the moon still rides high in the sky, the dew begins to settle on grass, plants and trees. Early morning dew is a great way to wake up the skin. It is high in oxygen, which means that it helps to replenish the skin and can even reduce spots and blemishes when used regularly. Furthermore, gathering the dew can become a ritual in itself and a time to commune with nature

and enjoy the energies of the liminal time between night and day. Although you can gather moon dew at any time of the year, May Day or 1st May was considered to be an especially magical time, as it signified the rebirth of spring, so May dew was said to have rejuvenating and youth-enhancing powers. It was also thought to have links with the faerie realms and their glamour, so to wash your face in May dew was said to give you a glowing complexion for the whole year.

The best time to gather moon dew is on a cool night, just before dawn. Take a clean sponge and walk around your garden or other natural space, gently wiping the sponge along leaves and flowers, to soak up the dew drops. The dew from roses was said to be especially beautifying. Once your sponge is damp with dew, use it to wipe over your face, neck, décolletage and anywhere else you wish to beautify. As you do so say;

By charm of moon and morning dew
I beautify myself anew.

You can repeat this ritual every day if you want to, incorporating it into a meditative early morning walk.

CHARGING WICCAN TRINKETS

Another way to use the moon's power is to charge your silver jewellery and Wiccan trinkets in the moonlight. This is best done on the night of the full moon. Silver is the metal most closely associated with the moon, so gather up any silver trinkets and magical charms you own and run them under the tap to cleanse them. Next lay them out on a windowsill, or place them in a glass container with a secure lid and leave them in the garden overnight, if your property is secure and safe from intruders. If you set your trinkets outside, make sure that magpies and squirrels can't steal them away! Leave your jewels in the light of the full moon to charge with lunar energy, then bring them in the next day. Each time your wear them you will know that you have the moon's radiance shining from your trinkets!

LUCKY WHITE HEATHER

Like most white flowering plants, white heather is associated with the moon and it is thought to bring good luck. In Scotland, it is traditional for a bride to carry a small sprig of white heather in her bridal bouquet and it is also used in the buttonholes of the groomsmen. It is a plant that was sacred to the Celtic druids, who viewed it as a plant of purity and cleansing. It was also used to make heather mead.

Even today, little sprigs of white heather are sold in Scottish tourist shops as lucky charms and wedding favours. Folklore states that white heather only grows where no blood has been spilt, which would explain its rarity in the Scottish Highlands, where many battles have been fought! It is also said to grow on the site of a faerie's grave. In some legends, sleeping on a bed of white heather was thought to render the sleeper invisible – a useful trick to know if you were a Jacobite hiding from the Redcoats!

There are several varieties of white blooming heather that grow well in large pots or as part of a larger flower bed, so this would be a very auspicious shrub to plant as part of a moon garden. It is a magical little moon-blessed plant, so if you ever come across it, be sure to carry a small spring or two away with you and good luck is sure to meet you.

THE MOON AS A WEATHER VANE

In another aspect of lunar folklore, the moon was considered to be a good indication of the weather. The most common example of this is the saying that a halo or ring around the moon would bring a hard frost in winter, while in summer it would bring rain.

The ring that sometimes forms around the moon is caused as the moonlight passes through ice crystals in the atmosphere, which from down here on earth, appears as a halo around the moon. It is a beautiful sight to behold and adds to the moon's mystery and charm. It is also a fairly accurate predictor of rain, frost or snow, depending on the season.

Other folklore states that a blue moon, which is the second full moon in a single calendar month, is a sign that a flood is due to happen, while if the tips of a new moon, or *horns* as they are sometimes known, are sharp and well defined, that would indicate that a period of stormy, windy weather is approaching. So it is always worth keeping an eye on the moon so that you know if you'll be needing an umbrella when you go out!

As you can see from this chapter, the moon has held our imagination captive for hundreds of years and we have a wealth of superstition and folklore as a result of our fascination with this bright lunar orb. Despite all that we know of her scientifically, she has still maintained an air of mystery and magic, drawing us into her light with promises of beauty, enchantment and luck. Just don't forget to bow to her every now and then.

CHAPTER THREE
LUNAR DEITIES

Since ancient times many of the planets and celestial bodies have been attributed to gods and goddesses. These deities are the personification of those planetary energies. They were invoked by practitioners who wanted to connect with those energies or request a special boon from the deity. The moon is no different and there are lots of deities associated with it. Because the moon is regarded as a feminine energy, most lunar deities are goddesses, but there are a few lunar gods too, as you will see in this chapter.

TRIPLE GODDESS

For pagans and witches, the moon represents the Triple Goddess, or the Three in One. The Triple Goddess is made up of the Maiden, the Mother and the Crone. The lunar cycle can be split among these three aspects of the goddess. From new to just before full moon is the time of the Maiden; full moon is the time of the Mother; waning to dark moon is the time of the Crone. Each aspect of the Triple Goddess represents different energies and can be invoked for different purposes.

The Maiden

The Maiden is the goddess of youthfulness, innocence and fresh starts. She can help you to get in touch with your inner child, or to adopt a more optimistic and youthful approach to life. She is the ingénue, for whom the world is a new discovery. She encourages us to try new things, take up new hobbies and experiences, to step bravely into new environments and situations. She is a breath of fresh air, the dawning of sexuality, fertility and romance. Her light is a silver crescent in the night sky, her pull is the incoming tide.

You might feel her energies as a certain restlessness, or itchy feet, during the new to waxing moon. Act on this restlessness and use her energies to try something new. Explore and go adventuring, book a holiday to a place you've never been before or take up a new hobby. All things new and uncharted come under the domain of the Maiden, so embrace it with a sense of exploration.

The Mother

The Mother represents the fruition of fertility, abundance, wealth, plenty, growth and expansion. She is the natural abundance of the harvest, the fruit of the orchard and the swelling seas of high tide. As the moon is round and full during the time of the Mother, it represents the growth of pregnancy, the anticipation of parenthood and the expectation of abundance in all things.

The Mother is all nurturing, encouraging you to perform acts of kindness to others and to practise self-care skills. New projects now begin to show considerable promise and you might begin to enjoy

the fruits of past labours during the time of the Mother phase. Her energies can be felt as a deep sense of contentment and faith that all will be well. She brings unexpected blessings, especially those that increase comfort and abundance, so look out for sudden windfalls and lovely invitations, as the Mother provides for you. Allow her to guide you towards a sense of peace and plenty.

The Crone

The Crone is the goddess of endings and darkness, of ebb tide and midnight. As the moon wanes to dark, its light shrinks to nothing, leaving the skies black as black for a short time. The Crone is perhaps the most misunderstood aspect of the Triple Goddess – she certainly seems to be the most feared by non-magical people! But their fears are unfounded, for the Crone is simply darkness and rest. She is the force that takes away all that no longer serves you and like the wind that strips the dead wood from trees, she is necessary to make room for new growth. She encourages you to let go and move on. She is the wisdom of the elder, the prophecy of the seer, the magic of the sorceress. She is powerful and strong, despite her aged appearance.

You might feel her energies as a sudden desire to declutter your home, or in a sharp lesson learnt. The Crone does not suffer fools gladly and her power will bring the life-lessons needed to make you stronger and more resilient, for she is a galvanizing force to be reckoned with. She is not without compassion though and she encourages you to take the rest that you need, when you need it,

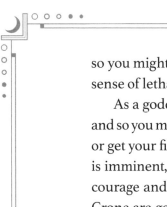

so you might sleep more during a waning or dark moon, or feel a sense of lethargy.

As a goddess of the Underworld she is associated with death, and so you might feel the need to make a will, take out life insurance or get your finances in order during her phase, not because death is imminent, but because she asks you to face the unknown with courage and to prepare for the unexpected. The energies of the Crone are good for banishing things from your life – bad habits, old patterns of behaviour, toxic friends etc. She expects you to make space for the blessings that are to come, so that you are ready to receive the fruit of the seeds that are sown during her darkness.

GUIDED MEDITATIONS

A guided meditation is a visualization technique. It is a great way to commune with the deities and energies of the moon. You will find lots of guided meditations in this book. It is usually best to record the meditation or have someone read it out loud to you. Lie down in a comfortable position and breathe deeply until you feel relaxed, then begin to envision the meditation below.

Maiden of the Moon Meditation

You find yourself standing in the middle of the Lunar Glen during the twilight hours of early dawn. The sun has yet to rise fully over the mountains and there is a new moon hanging in the grey pre-dawn sky. The air is fresh, with the promise of a warm day to come. You breathe in deeply, filling your lungs with cleansing air. It invigorates you and makes you feel ready for a day of adventure. Suddenly, you feel soft hands covering your eyes in a temporary blindfold. You hear a giggle just behind you, then a girl's voice whispers in your ear, "Guess who?" The hands disappear from your eyes and you swing around, only to see that there is no-one there. Again, you hear the giggle, but you cannot see who is laughing. Once more the voice travels upon the air, calling out "Catch me if you can!"

Out of nowhere, a bright spark of light bounces across the grass, dancing from place to place. The ball of silver light is no bigger than your fist and you watch in fascination as it dashes here and there, back and forth. Occasionally you hear the sound of giggling and it seems to be coming from the ball of light. You try to follow it and catch it, but it's too fast, leaving you gasping and laughing as the spark of light evades your grasp time and time again. It's like trying to catch the mist.

Then you begin to notice that whenever the ball of light touches the ground, fresh spring flowers are blossoming in a riot of colour. Before long the barren glen has become a wildflower meadow and you are standing amid thistles, daisies, clover, poppies, foxgloves and all manner of pretty blooms. The colours are vibrant and the flowers fill the air with their delicate scent. You gaze in wonder at the beauty that is blooming all around you.

The ball of light is now dancing all the way to the other side of the glen and you run to catch up. You hear the sound of a stream running by, and notice that the mountains are now blooming in purple heather, as the silver sphere dashes around, going higher and higher. You give up trying to follow, preferring to just sit at the bottom of the mountains and watch, captivated by the light. Once at the top, the tiny ball of light explodes into a sparkling waterfall that plunges down the mountain, into the stream below. You gasp in wonder at the powerful surge of pure white spray, falling straight down, like the tail of a unicorn.

Feeling like a child again, you call to the beam of light that is now hiding behind the waterfall, "Come out, come out wherever you are!" Another giggle ripples through the water. "Show yourself!" you say, growing impatient. Listening out for a response you hear the words "If you can name me, I will come to you." You stand up and reply "You are the Maiden of the Triple Goddess and I am a Follower of the Old Ways. I invoke you!" In a moment of pure magic, the waterfall freezes mid-flow and a pretty young maid

steps out onto the riverbank. She is in the first flush of womanhood, shapely and trim. Her silver-blonde hair falls in ripples to her waist and upon her head she wears a silver crown, with a waxing crescent moon at its centre. She wears a pure white gown of gauzy material that flutters in the breeze, like the wings of a butterfly. Around her wrists are living bracelets of wildflowers, signifying her connection to the earth and hanging on a delicate chain around her neck is a small silver star.

"Merry meet, Seeker of the Old Ones. I am the Maiden of the Moon and I come to bring you the light of opportunity and new growth. Embrace me!" She holds her arms open and you step into her embrace, soaking up her light and joyfulness, her vibrant enthusiasm for life. Stepping back, she takes both your hands in hers and begins to swing you around in circles. She throws her head back in laughter and you do the same, intoxicated by her charm and vitality. Suddenly she lets go and you both tumble to the grass, laughing like children.

After a moment she says, "I am the seed that you plant in the dark. I am the hope that lives in your heart. I am the playfulness you put to one side, thinking yourself too old to have fun, with too many responsibilities, but without such joy and adventure, life is barren and devoid of feeling. To know me is to embrace all that is new and unfamiliar. To embrace me is to live with the spirit of adventure." The

Maiden reaches up and removes her necklace, handing it over to you as she says, "Take this lucky star and keep it with you always. It is my gift to you – my gift of opportunity, good fortune and lucky chances. Go now Seeker of the Old Ones, back to your own realm, but look for me by the light of the waxing moon and know that I will always be smiling down upon you."

You fasten the charm around your neck and say farewell to the Maiden of the Moon, as you make your way back across the glen. When you feel ready, open your eyes and become aware of your surroundings, then go about your day.

Mother of the Moon Meditation

Once again you find yourself standing in the glen, as the full moon rides high in the sky and a myriad of stars twinkle and glitter above you. The night is chilly and a cool breeze rises to meet you as you make your way across the Lunar Glen. In the distance you see a light which echoes that of the moon above. As you make your way toward it you see that it comes from the round window of a croft house, set into the foot of the mountain, near the stream. The croft is pale in the moonlight, a whitewashed mirage of homeliness and comfort. Smoke curls from the chimney and the scent of cooking draws you in. The amber glow of candlelight spills from the portal window, illuminating a well-kept kitchen garden. Stepping close you notice an abundance of blackberries, crab apples, pears, turnips, carrots and potatoes, as well as other herbs and plants you are less familiar with. You pick a few blackberries and eat them, enjoying their sweet taste.

A pure white cat sits on the doorstep, watching you with emerald green eyes, bright in the moonlight. She rubs herself against the besom that leans against the door and purrs to get your attention. You bend to caress her soft fur and she pushes her head against your hand in pleasure and approval. Then you hear a warm voice say, "You seem to have made a friend! If my Luna likes you, then you may knock three times and enter." The voice seems to come from inside the house and so you knock solemnly three times upon the wooden

door, which swings wide open, though there is no-one there to greet you.

Stepping into the house you instantly feel at home. A cheerful fire casts a golden glow over the room and there are beeswax candles dotted around, their flickering flames creating dancing shadows on the walls, filling the room with the scent of warm honey. Luna the cat now sits upon the hearth rug, dozing in the heat from the flames that lick around a burning log. You notice that the table by the window has been set with two bowls and cups, almost as if you were expected, and the waft of cooking drifts across from the hearth.

"Please, make yourself at home." The same warm voice instructs you, as invisible hands push a comfy armchair up to the fireplace. You seat yourself and stretch out your legs to the hearth, wondering what is bubbling in the pot that hangs over the fire. Whatever it is it smells delicious and your mouth waters in anticipation. "You must be hungry," the voice comes again, closer this time and you watch in fascination as your invisible host dips a ladle into the pot and fills a bowl with something hot and steaming.

"Please, you're being so kind, why won't you show yourself to me?" you ask. "If you can name me, I will show myself to you," the voice responds, to which you reply without hesitation, "You are the Mother of the Triple Goddess and I am a Follower of the Old Ways. I invoke you!"

As soon as you have spoken the words of invocation, she appears before you, a comely, mature woman, pressing the bowl and a spoon into your hands. She is dressed in a deep red woollen gown, with a tartan shawl around her shoulders. Her hair is auburn, russet as the autumn leaves and it falls in waves to her shoulders. She wears a silver moon crown upon her head, with the full moon at its centre and you notice that she is pregnant, the bloom of her youth lost in the weight of the child she carries. She wears a seashell brooch signifying her connection to the tides and a silver apple charm hangs on a dainty chain around her neck.

"Merry meet and welcome, Seeker of the Old Ones. I am the Mother of the Moon and I bring you all the abundance you could ever need. Eat, drink and rest yourself, for the path you have chosen is a long one and you will need sustenance." She smiles as you dip the spoon into the soup she has made and you lift it to your lips to taste. It is hot and spicy, with a comforting aroma of herbs and vegetables. It nourishes you like no other soup you have ever tasted. You ask when her baby is due and again she smiles and says, "At Yuletide – mine is always a Yule babe. This little one is what keeps the world turning."

For a time, you sit in companionable silence as you eat the soup and rest a while. Then she says, "Worry not, Seeker, for there will always be plenty for you at my table. You will never know true hunger or want, for the riches I provide are abundant. I am the growth of your heart – aye, and your belly too if you're not careful!" she laughs and you chuckle as you savour the satisfied feeling of being well-fed. The Mother continues, "I am the growth of the seeds that you plant, my soil is fertile ground so be sure to plant only the seeds of your dreams, not those of your fears. I am the pride of your accomplishments and goals achieved. To know me is to know true homecoming and fulfilment. To embrace me is to live in the spirit of satisfaction, abundance and prosperity. Come now, Seeker of the Old Ones, you must be tired after your long journey. I'll give you a place to rest your head."

The Mother of the Moon picks up a candle and lights the way to a comfortable bed, built into the thickness of the croft wall. You lay down and she brings a warm woollen blanket and tucks you in gently. The bed is soft and cosy. It feels like the safest place you have ever known, as the Great Mother fusses around to make sure that you are settled and safe. Then she returns with a cup, which she presses into your hand. "Drink this potion before you sleep. 'Tis Mother's milk and nectar honey, with a sprinkling of cinnamon. It will help you to nod off and when you wake, you'll be back in your own realm."

Then the Mother reaches up and removes her necklace, handing it over to you as she says, "Take this silver apple and keep it with you always, as a promise of your future

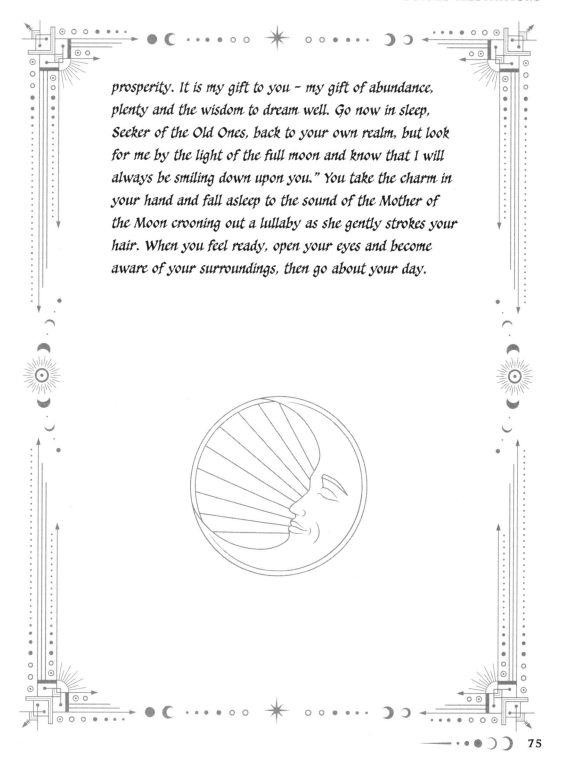

prosperity. It is my gift to you – my gift of abundance, plenty and the wisdom to dream well. Go now in sleep, Seeker of the Old Ones, back to your own realm, but look for me by the light of the full moon and know that I will always be smiling down upon you." You take the charm in your hand and fall asleep to the sound of the Mother of the Moon crooning out a lullaby as she gently strokes your hair. When you feel ready, open your eyes and become aware of your surroundings, then go about your day.

Crone of the Moon Meditation

You find yourself once more standing in the Lunar Glen. The night is almost black, with only the last sliver of the waning moon hanging in the starry sky. Your warm breath clouds in the frozen air and the frostbitten grass crunches beneath your feet as you walk. Although the glen is now familiar to you, the pitch dark makes everything look different and you feel a little lost. You set off walking, trying to find the comfort of the croft house, but there is only a tangle of thistles where it once stood. Dejected you turn away and begin to walk back the way you came.

As you walk, your head bowed against the cold wind, you suddenly hear the cawing sound of a raven, and looking up you see a dark shadow, looping and swooping through the air – a darker shape amid the black night sky. The raven seems to be trying to get your attention, swooping in towards you before flying off again with a loud caw. You wonder why a raven would be flying in the middle of the night. It comes closer this time, cawing right in your face before ascending the sky once more. It's as if it wants you to follow it and so you do, treading carefully across the rocky floor of the winter glen, so as not to slip on the icy surface.

The raven flies ahead of you, and in time you find yourself at the foot of a rocky crag. Here the bird swoops low and disappears into a cleft in the rock face. You follow, squeezing between two walls of damp rock and find yourself in a tunnel. It is even colder here and you shiver, wondering what sort of creatures might live in this dark dwelling. Rats, bats? Your heart is thumping and you turn to go back out of the cleft and into the familiarity of the glen, when you hear a cackle of laughter, echoing raw like the raven's cries, followed by the words "Yes, run away, why don't you?! That's all they ever do. No time for an old bird like me, no consideration for what I might know. Only the wise will ever come to know me. Only the brave dare to follow where I lead, but you, no...you run at the first hint of darkness. Off you go then. See if I care! Be off with you and I'll just keep my secrets to myself, so I will!"

Intrigued and challenged, you step deeper into the tunnel. A dim light shines up ahead and you notice that there are indeed bats hanging upside down from the roof of the tunnel. You fear they might swarm and so you tread softly, trying not to disturb their sleep. "Yes, try not to wake the little ones – they have a taste for blood," the voice says, almost as if someone is reading your thoughts. You take a deep breath to calm your nerves and move slowly toward the light at the far end of the tunnel. A toad hops across your path with a croak, startling you and stopping you in your tracks. What else lives here?

As you approach the light, you begin to feel a warmth that thaws out your frozen face and fingers. You hear the spitting of a fire and when the tunnel turns a corner it opens out into a large cave. There in the centre, a fire burns in a circle of stones. A tripod of branches is set up over the fire and a cauldron hangs above the flames. You dread to think what might be cooking within the pot. "Eye of newt and toe of frog, eh?" the voice comes again, but you cannot see the speaker. "You've been reading too many stories!"

Summoning all your courage you ask, "May I share your fire this cold and frosty night?"

"Share my fire?!" the voice rasps. "Not brought so much as a stick of kindling and it wants to share my fire, that I toiled to gather and build and burn. What will you give, to share my fire? What sacrifice will you make to know my warmth and light?"

You feel in your pockets and find the silver apple charm, given to you by the Mother of the Moon, as a pledge of future abundance and plenty. Whoever lives in this cave seems to have more need of it than you do and so you hold it up in the light of the fire and say, "All I have is this charm of plenty. It is yours, if you will allow me to warm myself at your hearth."

"Step closer then and let me see it." You move toward the fire and say, "I would like to see to whom I am indebted. Will you reveal yourself to me?"

"If you can name me, I will reveal myself to you," the voice responds, to which you reply without hesitation, "You are the Crone of the Triple Goddess and I am a Follower of the Old Ways. I invoke you!"

As soon as you have spoken the words of invocation there is a shuffling behind you and turning you come face to face with the Crone. She is old and bent, her face grizzled with the years she carries. She wears a black tattered gown, festooned in raven feathers, and a white shawl that looks as if it might be made of lace or cobwebs, depending on the light. Her hair is long and silver grey, falling to her shoulders and upon her brow is the crown of the waning moon. Her left eye is clouded white, while her right eye is dark as the raven. She examines the charm you offer her for a moment, then she places it back in your hand, closes your fingers around it and says, "Your kindness is noted, Seeker of the Old Ones, but do not give away your prosperity so lightly. I didn't give it to you so that you could squander it!"

"You gave me this charm? That was you, in the croft?" The Crone nods and says, "'Twas many moons ago, but yes, I gave you that charm, and the one before it. Time passes, but I hoped that one day you would seek me out again. Come, share my fire and enjoy a cup of warm cheer with me." She pats your hand, as friendly now as a loving grandmother, as welcoming as she had been fearsome before. She hobbles to the fireside and ladles something from the cauldron into a cup and hands it to you. It is a steaming liquid, ruby red as blood which you hesitate to drink, until you notice that the Crone is watching you. You take a cautious sip. The liquid is hot and warms you through. It tastes familiar, but you cannot place it, until the Crone says, "Mulled wine and honey mead. It's good for keeping out the cold. Drink up, Seeker, and merry meet again."

The two of you sit in companionable silence as you sip the mulled wine and thaw out by the fire. After a time, the Crone speaks. "I knew you'd come back eventually, but I wasn't sure you'd be bold enough to find me and look me in the eyes. Not everyone can. Many people never get to know me. They fear me, for I am the witches they burnt at the stake. They flee from me, for I am the frailty of old age and the death that awaits. I am the elder years they try to avoid thinking about. But I am also wisdom, forbearance, darkness and rest.

I am the powerful magic of a long-lived witch. I am the depths of winter and the darkness of midnight on a waning moon. I am all these things and more. To know me is to be unafraid of the dark, to embrace me is to embrace your own mortality and that of your loved ones. I am fearsome because they project their fears onto me. I don't pretend to be easy company, but I am necessary. I strip away the dead wood to make way for new growth, new life, transformation and rebirth. But my time this moon is almost up. Take this." The crone reaches around her neck with trembling hands, and removes a silver cauldron charm, hanging on a delicate chain. "This is the charm of transformation and rebirth. It

is yours now and it will take you back to your own realm in due course. But first, help me to my bed, Seeker, and stay with me until the end."

You help the old lady to a ragged bed in the corner of the cave and tuck her under a blanket. "Fear not, Seeker," she says, "for I will not be far away. Look for me in the waning moon, where I will always be watching over you." With a bowed head, you sit by her side holding her hand and stroking back her hair, just as she once did for you in the croft, until her dim eyes close for the last time. As the moon in the glen turns dark, the Crone breathes her last breath and disappears. In her place rests a tiny ball of light, newly formed and tremulous.

When you feel ready, open your eyes and become aware of your surroundings, then go about your day.

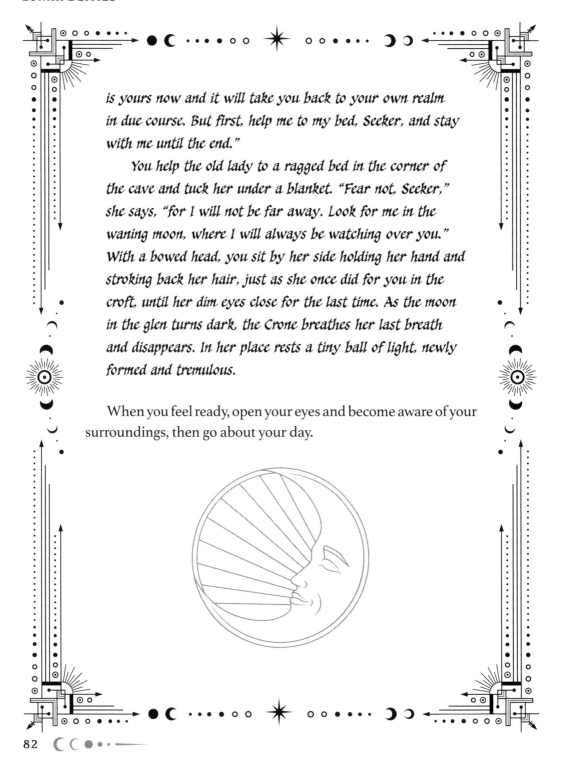

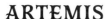

ARTEMIS

The Greek deity Artemis is one of the most well-known moon goddesses. She is associated with the hunt, carrying a bow and arrows and linked to deer, hares and hounds, which are all her totem animals. The crescent moon is regarded as her bow in the night sky. Artemis is a virgin goddess who maintained her chastity. She is seen as a self-sufficient deity of great independence and one who finds her own path. The Greek Priestesses of the Moon were also expected to remain virgins and Artemis was extremely vengeful if any of them were abused, or fell from grace in any way. Artemis was said to have helped her mother give birth to her twin brother Apollo, whilst she was only a baby herself, so she is also associated with childbirth too, despite being a virgin goddess. She can be invoked for spells of independence, chastity and childbirth.

ARIANRHOD – SILVER WHEEL

Arianrhod is a Welsh goddess associated with the moon and sometimes known as the Lady of the Silver Wheel. This Wheel is thought to represent the turning of time and the weaving of fate and destiny. Arianrhod's silver oar wheel was also the means by which the dead were carried into the afterlife and she is known as a goddess of reincarnation. She is linked with the North Star and therefore with guidance during times of trauma. Like many Celtic goddesses, Arianrhod was skilled in needlecraft, particularly weaving and she is the weaver of the cosmic web. Mythology tells us that she lived in a castle in the polar region of stars, known as

Caer Sidi and that she rode a snowy white chariot through the heavens to watch over the tides that she governed. Her feast day falls on the 2nd of December each year and so she is also a goddess of winter. The appearance of the Aurora Borealis is a sign that she is near and her totem animal is a pure white owl. Although not one of the virgin goddesses, Arianrhod was an independent deity who would not share her power with a consort. She can be called upon for guidance, autonomy and winter moon magic.

SELENE

Selene was one of the original Greek Titan goddesses, which were the most powerful deities of all and regarded as being the creators of the universe. Selene was a moon goddess and she held dominion over the night sky and the heavens. In the Roman pantheon her counterpart's name is simply Luna. In Wicca she is often worshipped during the Esbat rituals of new and full moons. In mythology Selene is said to drive her silver chariot, pulled by white horses or unicorns, across the sky each night, casting out dreams and blessings as she goes. Selene fell in love with Endymion, a young shepherd boy. She cast a sleeping spell upon him so that she might visit him in secret each night, without revealing herself to a mortal man. Because of this, Selene is also regarded as being a goddess of romance and of difficult or secret love affairs. Invoke her for sweet dreams, new romance, manifestation and general good blessings.

SIN

Sin, also known as Suen, Nanna or Nannar, is the Mesopotamian god of the moon. He was revered in ancient times throughout the Eastern civilizations, including Babylon and Arabia. His totem animal was the bull and all cattle fell under his protection, as did the herdsmen who watched over the herd. Sin was the father of the better-known goddess, Inanna or Ishtar, who was known as the Queen of Heaven. She is a significant figure in Wicca.

MANI

Interestingly, in Norse mythology the deities for sun and moon are subverted, with Mani being the god of the moon and his sister, Sol, being the goddess of the sun. Both Mani and Sol were fathered by a mortal man who was so taken by their good looks that he named them after the moon and sun. This made the Norse gods very angry and to punish him for his arrogance, they placed his children high in the heavens, forcing them to forever guide the orbs they were named for across the sky.

Because he is of mortal parentage, Mani is sometimes considered to be the original *man in the moon*. While there are several variations of this folktale, in most versions the man in the moon is someone who was banished from earth for some sort of wrongdoing, so far from being a forgotten lunar god, Mani is actually a celebrated icon in nurseries all over the world!

FREYA

Another Norse deity who is strongly associated with the moon is Freya, who was one of the most important goddesses of the Norse pantheon. Freya was the goddess of beauty, love, war, magic and witchcraft. It is through her link with magic and witchcraft that she is associated with the moon, particularly the full moon, as it is the most auspicious time for spell casting. Her totem animals are cats and she is often depicted in a silver or gold chariot, being drawn by a pair of wildcats. She was invoked as a goddess of fertility throughout Scandinavia. After making a deal with the god Odin, Freya could claim the souls of half the number of warriors who died in battle and thus she is a death goddess too.

CERRIDWEN

Celtic goddess of the moon, Cerridwen is also linked to inspiration, transformation, creativity and wisdom gained through experience. She is sometimes called The Keeper of the Cauldron, for she presides over a magical cauldron that can bring the dead back to life. As a result, she is associated with the cycle of life, death and rebirth. Her totem animal is a pure white sow and represents fertility. She is a patron of poets, writers, artists, musicians and bards. Call on her for all issues of creativity, fertility and inspiration.

KHONSU

Khonsu, meaning *the traveller*, is the Egyptian god of the moon and time. He was said to guide and protect anyone who had to travel by night, watching over them like a guardian. For this reason, he is known as a pathfinder and a defender, similar to Saint Christopher of Christian belief. He was associated with healing and fertility. He is the master of the night and a powerful god to invoke for matters of protection, guidance and guardianship, so if you have to work the night shift he is the one to call on.

As you can see there are lots of goddesses and gods that are linked to the moon and the lunar cycle. Although they are all lunar deities, each one has their own special attributes and totems, so do your research and read up on the deities which interest you the most. When you have decided which lunar deity you would like to work with in ritual, use the following invocation to call on their power.

CHARM OF INVOCATION

To invoke your preferred deity, stand in the light of the appropriate moon phase, hold your hands high above your head and say the following charm of invocation. When you have completed the invocation, you are ready to make magic and cast spells with the aid of your chosen lunar deity.

> ------------(name deity) I call you
> By silver light of ancient moon,
> Deity of lunar grace
> I invoke your blessings for this magic boon,
> I invite your presence into this space,
> Grant to me thy silver light
> Share with me thy gentle glow
> Give unto me your wisdom bright
> As your ever-changing power I come to know
> So mote it be.

When you have worked your ritual and completed all the spells and divinations you want to cast, release the deity you called by saying the following words.

> Blessed be -----------(name deity)
> I give thanks for your presence and release you.
> Go in peace and love
> Blessed be.

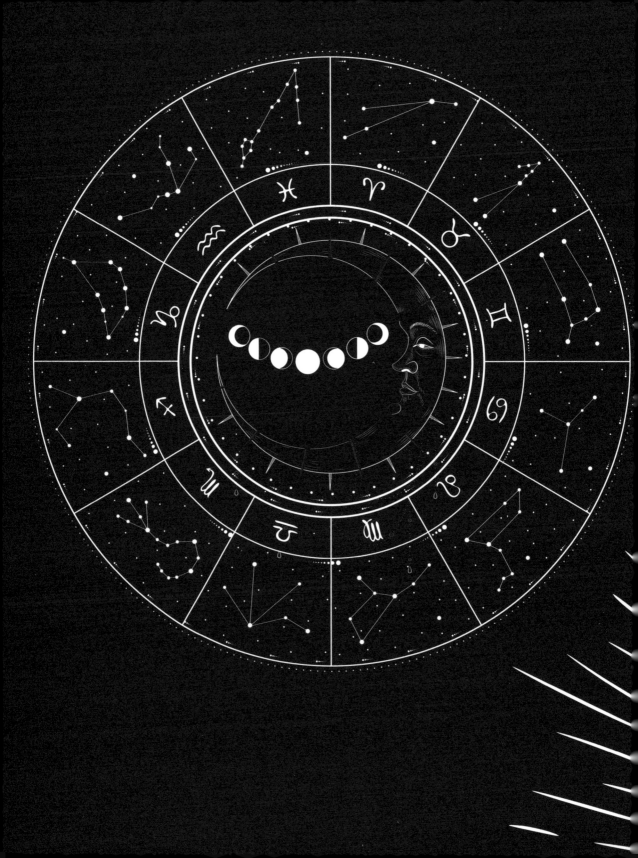

CHAPTER FOUR
MOON SIGNS

he moon's orbit takes it through all the signs of the zodiac, switching from one sign to the next roughly every two and a half days. Each new moon always falls within the current zodiac sign, while the full moon of that month falls into the opposing sign on the zodiac wheel. For instance, if we were currently in the zodiac sign of Scorpio roughly October 23rd – November 22nd, then the new moon of that period would also be in Scorpio, while the full moon would be in the opposing sign of Taurus. This effectively means that the moon casts two different influences over us throughout the sign of Scorpio, so we feel a boost of Scorpio energies during the new moon and a strong influx of Taurean energy during the full moon. This same pattern is true as we pass through all the zodiac signs of the year.

Discovering your moon sign can be as complicated as you want it to be. To pinpoint the exact place the moon was in when you were born, you would need to know your time of birth and have a birth chart drawn up, but in simple terms, your moon sign influence is the one opposite the zodiac sign you were born into. So if you were born into the sun sign of Aquarius then your moon sign influence would be Leo. Moon sign energy can influence all of us, but it is especially powerful when either the new or full moon is in your own zodiac sign. Let's take a look at the moon signs of the zodiac and how their influences might affect you.

MOON IN ARIES

Aries is a fire sign, ruled by the planet Mars, the god of war, so expect fiery tempers, short fuses and a tendency towards confrontation when this moon sign is in play. This is a great time to stand up for yourself and make your feelings known, as Aries energy surrounds you and helps you to feel strong and bold. Take care not to let this tip over into a feeling of invincibility, or you could find yourself out of your depth.

New Moon – Use the bold energy of an Aries new moon to put your own needs first and take time for yourself.

Full Moon – When the full moon is in Aries keep your eyes peeled for new opportunities coming your way and be sure to make the most of them.

MOON IN TAURUS

The earth sign of Taurus is ruled by the planet Venus, the goddess of love and beauty. This moon sign influences people to take better care of themselves with self-love rituals and pampering. It can even lead you towards a new relationship, shining a light upon a new love interest or deepening the bond between long-term lovers. However, Taurus also has a no-nonsense approach to life, so practical expressions of affection are more likely during this time, rather than big romantic gestures.

New Moon – This is a time for slowing down, so don't be surprised if circumstances force you into a slower pace of life for a short time. Use this time to pamper and recharge.

Full Moon – Taurus energy is all about stability, so use this influence to increase your levels of overall security, be this financial or personal. Remember that building a sense of security around yourself is also a form of self-care and take responsibility for your personal safety and home security.

Aries

Taurus

MOON IN GEMINI

The air sign of Gemini is ruled by the planet Mercury, the god of communication, and this sign is certainly known for its flamboyant energies. When the moon is in Gemini, it is basically calling you out to play, filling your calendar with events and nights out. This moon sign is the party-going influencer and the energies at work right now tend to make people feel adventurous and generally more playful. Take care though, because too much Gemini energy can lower inhibitions, which leads to recklessness and taking greater risks.

New Moon – Time to make plans with friends, collaborate with colleagues on a big project or set up a new website. Communication is the key and you could find yourself going out every night or spending hours on the phone chatting.

Full Moon – Use this moon to do some networking and expand your circle of friends. It's always fun to meet new people and try new things. Monitor your socializing however, because if you burn the candle at both ends you could end up burnt out altogether.

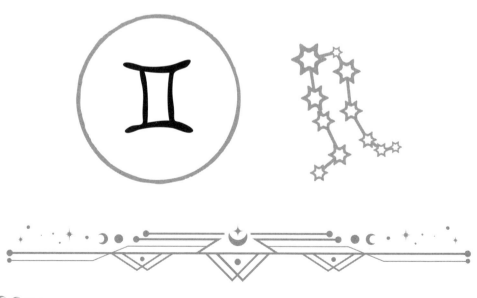

MOON IN CANCER

The water sign of Cancer is ruled by the moon itself, giving a double whammy of lunar energies and heightening emotions during this moon sign. Emotions tend to run high under this influence, so don't be surprised if you feel hyper sensitive or a little tearful at this time. Just as the water of the tides ebb and flow, your emotions might be up and down for a while, leading to a sense of fragility and vulnerability. Cancerian energy is known for hiding emotions beneath a hard shell, but when the moon is in Cancer, you can expect all those hidden, repressed emotions to come to the fore.

New Moon – This is a good time to retreat into your shell and spend some time in hibernation, away from the hustle and bustle of life. Go within and reflect on the emotions this moon sign has brought up for you.

Full Moon – Understand that a hard shell doesn't only protect you from the hard knocks of life, it can also be a barrier to all the good things too. Use this time to learn how to be vulnerable in a safe way, perhaps with a therapist or trusted friend. Open up and explore your inner mental landscapes.

Gemini

Cancer

MOON IN LEO

The fire sign of Leo is ruled by the sun, making this another flamboyant sign. Unlike the party atmosphere of a Gemini moon however, a Leo moon uses this flamboyance for furthering ambition and for getting noticed for all the right reasons, both professionally and personally. This moon sign influence will make you shine! It will draw you out into the spotlight and encourage you to be your best self. A Leo moon brings out the leadership in all of us and you might be called upon to take charge of a situation or give a keynote speech or presentation at work. The lion likes to shake out his golden mane for all to see!

New Moon – This is a good time to start fleshing out your ambitions and mapping out a path to achieve your objectives. Do you need to apply for a course or a promotion, attend interviews or auditions or organize a networking event? Use this lunar energy to project yourself forwards into your dreams, one step at a time.

Full Moon – Be bold and follow your heart. What sparks the joy in your life, what gets you fired up, what are you enthusiastic about? Use this phase to act on these spiritual prompts and follow your bliss.

MOON IN VIRGO

The earth sign of Virgo is ruled by the planet Mercury, god of communication. These lunar energies will keep you busy all month if you let them because Virgo is the sign of hustle culture, perfectionism, organization and personal achievement. At its best, a Virgo moon will help you to declutter and reorganize your entire house, but at its worst it will draw you into nit-picking perfectionism and procrastination because you cannot do something perfectly first time round. Nothing is perfect and while you might keep telling yourself that there is always room for improvement, eventually this kind of mentality can start to work against you, meaning that you never finish anything!

New Moon; beware of taking on too much at this time. Stick to one or two things that you know you can get done to a high standard and still have free time to decompress. Beware of becoming too critical, both of yourself and others.

Full Moon; this is the time when perfectionism can go into overdrive! This is great if you need a boost of motivation as it can drive you to achieve, but if you are already a high achiever then watch out for hubris and a *save the world* mentality creeping in. Treat yourself to a day off!

Leo

Virgo

MOON IN LIBRA

The air sign of Libra is ruled by the planet Venus, goddess of love. When this moon sign is in charge you might be tempted to try and bring more balance to your life, perhaps by prioritizing love and family over your career, for instance. However, a classic Libran trait is that of indecision. They cannot seem to choose between two or more options, often preferring to have their cake and eat it, which can lead to fractious relationships and eventual isolation. The need to compartmentalize life is also a Libran trait, as they try to separate out aspects of their life and contain them in boxes. Eventually, though, all the contents spill out and they find themselves in a mess of their own design! Watch out for these traits when the moon is in Libra. By all means use the energies to bring more balance into your life, but be careful not to over-compartmentalize. Accept that life is messy at times, different aspects of your world will bleed into one another and that is as it should be. Containment will only work for so long.

New Moon – Practise your decision-making skills! If you can hone this vital life skill you will naturally bring about more balance because you will no longer be torn between several options, plus you'll feel more in control as the decision will not be made for you by circumstance.

Full Moon – Seek forgiveness from those who might have been hurt by your indecisiveness in the past and set the scales of justice right. Love triangles are common when Libra energy is at play, so

look to make amends for any hurt you might have caused and to heal your own emotional wounds. Emotional balance is just as important as life balance.

MOON IN SCORPIO

As a water sign, Scorpio is ruled by the planets Pluto and Mars, bringing influences of death and rebirth from Pluto, and also war and conflict from Mars. This is a heady, potent mix, meaning that when the moon is in Scorpio, tensions can run high and intense emotions are frequently in play. These lunar energies can lead to an existential crisis. Reflecting on the deeper meaning of life, death, afterlife and the overall meaning of your own personal existence and value is common at this time. A Scorpio moon is intense, brutal, seductive, overwhelming, enticing and obsessive. It is a deep dive into humanity and what it means to be alive. It's big,

Libra

Scorpio

powerful stuff and it can have a profound influence on people. At best these lunar energies teach resilience and robustness, at worst they can lead to deep feelings of melancholia and worthlessness. This is not a moon to mess with, but one to court gently, with both passion and compassion.

New Moon – This is the time to live in the moment, to live with passion! Allow life to seduce you. Be bold, be sexy and use your charms. Take hold of your power and make the most of it.

Full Moon – Embrace new experiences but be aware that Scorpio has some very dark energies which can lead you into an even darker place if you are not careful. Depression, addiction, manipulation, risk-taking and so on, can all come into play during this moon. Focus instead on the passion and vibrancy of Scorpio energies, let go of the past and feed your desires in a safe way.

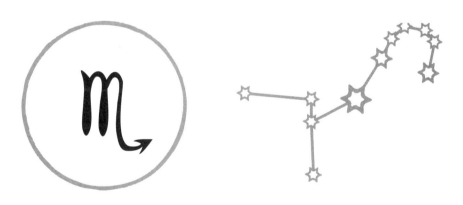

MOON IN SAGITTARIUS

Fire sign Sagittarius is ruled by the planet Jupiter, god of thunder and the sky. When the moon is in this sign you may feel the urge to go on an adventure, go exploring or take a trip somewhere you've never been before. A Sagittarius moon is all about taking calculated risks and trying new things. It is not about being reckless, which is more of a Scorpio moon trait. Instead, this moon suggests that something new is calling to you, something which will expand your horizons and your world view.

New Moon – This is the time to change up your habits and create some new ones. Learn a new language, start a hobby or join a group or sports team. Have fun and enjoy the spirit of adventure that this lunar energy brings.

Full Moon – Now is the time to break out of your comfort zone! Go travelling, volunteer for a charity, spread your wings and see what happens. The archer's energy can help you to shoot for the moon, so aim as high as you can.

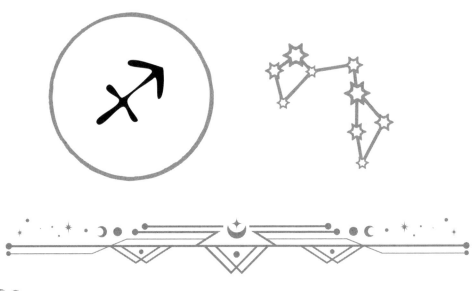

MOON IN CAPRICORN

The earth sign of Capricorn is ruled by the planet Saturn, bringer of dark emotions, big life lessons and melancholia. When the moon is in this sign it can bring with it the need to excel. It influences people to press ahead, set goals, make plans, work harder and increase their self-discipline. The moon in Capricorn is a great motivator, so if this is your moon sign you are likely to be a very self-driven and determined character, who is probably a high achiever. The Capricorn moon makes you want to manifest all your wildest ambitions to the highest degree.

New Moon – This is the time to decide in detail exactly what it is that you want from your life. Set your goals and start making plans to achieve them.

Full Moon – Remind yourself how far you've already come! Give yourself a pat on the back and celebrate all that you have already achieved, before you look towards your long-term goals for the future. Remember to show gratitude for what you have.

Sagittarius

Capricorn

MOON IN AQUARIUS

Flighty air sign Aquarius is ruled by the planets Uranus and Saturn, bringing energies of extremes and breakouts from Uranus, along with Saturn's traits of life lessons and melancholia. When the moon is in Aquarius you might act irrationally or impetuously, without thinking far enough ahead to see what the consequences of your actions might be. This is the rebellious moon, the one which can make people act spontaneously, childishly and selfishly. Reality is an inconvenience; consequences are for other people to have to deal with. The lunar energies at this time can make you restless, flitting from pillar to post, bouncing off one thing straight into the next, be this in your relationships, jobs or hobbies. You might be tempted to let other people clean up your mess, or abdicate all sense of personal responsibility. An Aquarius moon carries with it a sense of unreality and a wilful ignorance of the damage done, so look before you leap!

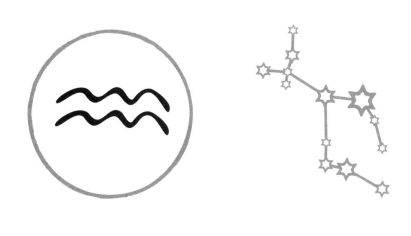

New Moon – Freedom is your watchword, so embrace your liberty and have fun! Make your wildest visions your reality – take a flying lesson, go on a speedboat, learn to ride a motorcycle. Give your rebellious spirit a safe, controlled outlet before it gets you into trouble!

Full Moon – This is the time of breakthroughs, breakouts and sometimes breakdowns. You might suddenly realize that you hate your job and want to leave, or that your relationship is over. When the need to break out takes hold, make sure that you do a risk assessment and check your facts before you act on impulse. Aquarius energy is a dynamic force so try to keep a level head.

MOON IN PISCES

Water-loving sign Pisces is ruled by the planet Neptune, god of the sea. Still waters run deep and when the moon is in this sign you are more likely to be ruled by your emotions than by logic or common

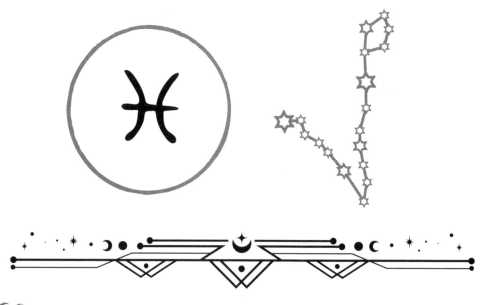

Aquarius

Pisces

sense. A Pisces moon can be a flat calm, a tsunami or a combination of the two. Little things might trigger a storm of emotion during this time and your empathic abilities may be heightened, meaning that you pick up on other people's emotions as well as your own and it can be difficult to draw the line between the two. Emotional hangovers are common at this time and you might feel more tired than usual, or have more meaningful dreams.

New Moon – Use all that emotional energy by channelling it into a creative endeavour, such as painting, journaling, composing music or poetry. Creativity can be a great balm for the emotions, offering a positive outlet so that they don't fester. Find an artistic way to get your emotions out and pin them down in a creative way.

Full Moon – Strengthen your boundaries! All that empathy can have a negative impact on your own well-being, so make sure that you reinforce your personal boundaries during this moon.

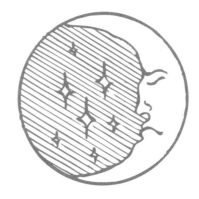

CHAPTER FIVE
MOON MANIFESTATION

All magic is a kind of manifestation because you are attempting to bring into being something that wasn't in your reality prior to casting the spell. You can also use magic to banish something which no longer serves you and in this sense you are manifesting a void that you can fill with something better. Witches have always manifested in tune with the moon and we cast our spells in accordance with certain phases to bring about specific results.

The moon teaches us to have patience, even when casting for our deepest desires. It is a visual reminder that magic can take time. A general rule of thumb is that smaller spells take approximately one full lunar cycle to manifest, while bigger spells may take several months. So if you were to cast for a windfall on the new moon, you might find yourself with a pay rise by the time the next new moon comes around. Likewise, if you were casting to move house or start a family on the full moon, it could be six full moons or more before this goal manifests in your life. The bigger the goal, the longer it takes, but the moon is a constant companion as you wait for the manifestation to occur, offering you a visual cue to stay positive and keep affirming your success.

LIKE ATTRACTS LIKE

In magic, like attracts like, so what you focus on the most is what you are pulling into your life. This happens whether you are aware of it or not and it is the reason why it pays to be positive. Negative habits and thought patterns, feelings of low self-worth, disparaging self-talk and so on, can all work to bring more negative circumstances your way. Fortunately, the opposite is also true, so surrounding yourself with positive people, habits and thought processes will bring more positive circumstances towards you. Be mindful of the energies that you are sending out into the world because that is exactly the kind of energy that will come back to you. Be optimistic, positive, gentle and kind, and that is what you will attract.

DECLARE YOUR INTENTIONS TO THE MOON

Making a declaration is a powerful thing. There is a reason that people remember the first time their partner said "I love you" – it's because this is a powerful declaration of an emotional bond. There is also a reason why you often say it back – because like attracts like! With this in mind, declaring your intentions to the moon can have a deep impact on your chances of success, because you are putting your goal out into the universe, confiding in the moon like an old friend.

Think of something that you want to achieve in the next month. It could be that you want to sign up to a new class, or start a new hobby, make a new friend etc. Once you have your intention in mind, go outside on the night of the full moon. Look up at the bright orb in the sky and breathe in her energies, then state your intention out loud or in your head. For example, you might say something like, *"Mother moon I greet you and welcome your light, I set my intention to take up dance classes this night."*

Now as you watch the moon move through her cycle, she will remind you each night to follow through on your intention, so that by the time she is full once more, you are already attending dance classes and living the reality of that ambition. You can repeat this process for any goal. Just remember that bigger goals will take longer than a month to manifest.

MOON MAPPING

Another technique for manifesting with the moon is that of moon mapping. This is great for larger goals and is a good way to maintain focus and motivation. Think of a large goal that you would like to achieve, then break it down into smaller achievable tasks. Write out the phases of the moon on a sheet of paper and alongside each phase, plot out the tasks of your goal, in alignment with that moon phase. So if you wanted to start a new business, for example, your moon map might look something like this.

☾ *New Moon* – Write a business plan.

☾ *Waxing Moon* – Set up a website or scout for premises.

☾ *Full Moon* – Apply for a business loan, open a business bank account and register as self-employed for tax purposes.

☾ *Waning Moon* – Hand in your notice or reduce your hours at your current job and clear out anything that isn't in alignment with your new business plan.

☾ *Dark Moon* – Conduct market research and product development for your business.

☾ *New Moon* –Start trading.

☾ This type of time structuring means that you are drawing upon the energies of the moon that are in alignment with the tasks you need to perform. You can use a moon map for any goal and you can expand the time scale so that you are mapping out several months of lunar cycles, rather than just the one as given in the example above. The beauty of this is that the lunar cycle keeps you on track with your plans, be they long or short term.

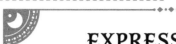

EXPRESS GRATITUDE

Gratitude is a vital component of all magic and manifestation. Lack of gratitude can derail your magic in a heartbeat. Demonstrating that you appreciate what you already have will ensure that more comes to you. Traditionally the full moon is a propitious time to offer your gratitude to the universe, but ideally you should show that you are grateful on a daily basis. Gratitude is an active pursuit, not a passive one. Here are some ideas for demonstrating gratitude.

☾ Keep a gratitude journal and write down 3-5 things that you are grateful for each night before you go to sleep. What did the day bring that you particularly enjoyed?

☾ Light a stick of incense and allow it to burn on your moon altar as an offering of gratitude to the universe for all that you have.

☾ Donate to those in need, as this is a way of acknowledging that you are fortunate enough to have an excess. Clothes, books, baby things – whatever you have an abundance of, go through and donate some things to charity.

☾ Tithe to a charity by making a financial contribution each month to an organization you care about.

☾ Offer your time and do some volunteering. You could visit a nursing home and spend time with the elderly, or offer to babysit for a friend so she can have some downtime.

☾ Send a thank-you note to someone who has helped you in some way.

☾ Cook a meal for someone.

☾ Feed the wildlife by putting out bird feeders and nuts for squirrels etc.

☾ Pick up litter to show gratitude for the beautiful planet we are lucky enough to call home.

☾ Show gratitude for freedom and security by assisting military veterans. Offer your time to service charities or buddy up with an ex-serviceman or woman in your area.

☾ Appreciate what you have and the people who surround you.

☾ Know that gratitude is the fastest way to experience the manifestation of your goals.

A LUNAR SPELL TO MANIFEST A DREAM

If there is something that you have wanted for a long time, then casting a little bit of magic can help to pull it toward you. Is there something that you have almost given up on, believing that you are not meant to have it? Or it could be that your wish was almost granted, only to be snatched away again soon afterwards. Take heart, because this is a sign that your dream is coming to you and you just need to have a little more patience. You can use this magic to draw it closer. On a new moon, begin by writing your wish on a piece of paper and then keep the paper close to your heart for seven nights. Then as the moon waxes towards full, burn the spell paper in a cauldron as you say:

My heartfelt wish is in this fire
I call on magic to lift me higher
And manifest my true desire.

Let the ashes cool down and then scatter them to the four winds to release the spell out into the universe.

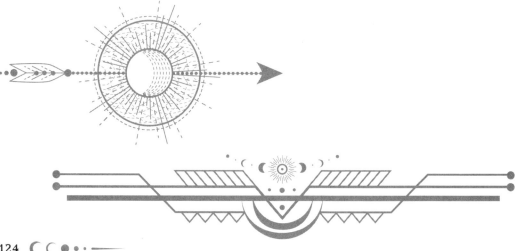

HOW TO MAKE WISH-FULFILMENT INCENSE

Burning incense is an ancient way of honouring and petitioning the gods and you can use this technique in your rituals to honour the moon. Burning incense on a daily basis is one of the easiest types of spells to cast, providing you do so with intention. It's quick, it's easy and it takes very little time to complete the ritual. It is also something that you can easily add into your evening routine when you come home from work, so that you get a touch of magic into your day.

Making your own incense means that your rituals become more potent, because you can charge the incense with a specific intention as you make it, in this case that of wish-fulfilment to help make your dreams come true.

You will need a clean empty jar and lid, a mortar and pestle and the following dried herbs and spices – mint, basil, lavender, calendula, tea leaf and cinnamon. These are great for manifestation spells because they are said to bring luck, good fortune and opportunity.

On the night of the new moon, place a teaspoon of each into the mortar and grind them together with the pestle using a clockwise motion. As you do so imagine that this incense will carry your wishes directly to the moon and her deities, who will hear your desires and help them to manifest in your life. Once the incense resembles a fine powder, pour it into the jar and label it Wish Fulfilment Incense. Leave the jar on a windowsill where it can soak

up the moon's energies for a full lunar cycle, by which time it will be ready to use in your spell-craft.

There are several ways that you can use this incense in your magic. You can burn a pinch or two on a charcoal block as this is more traditional, or you could use it as a scattering powder and sprinkle it on your doorstep, windowsills and around your home to draw your intentions towards you. In addition, you can anoint a candle with lunar oil and then roll it in the incense to give a powerful boost to your candle rituals.

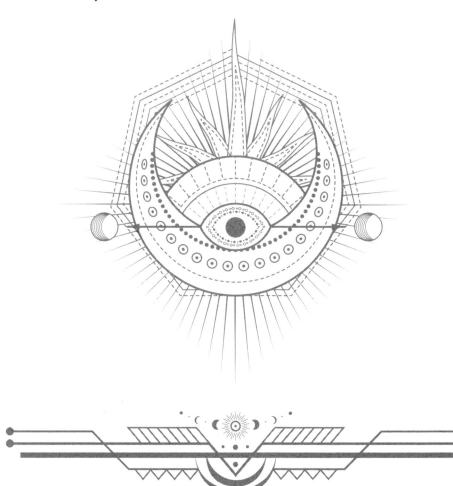

THE DARK SIDE OF THE MOON

The dark side of the moon is the side of the moon that faces away from the earth. It is associated with the unknown, the mysterious, spiritual rest, dark psychology, shadow work and reassessing your life. In terms of manifestation, the dark side of the moon invites you to explore your mental landscape, identify any blocks that are standing in your way and fine-tune your inner circle. This lunar influence is suggestive of deep personal reflection and raises the question, *Where are you heading and who are you taking along for the ride?*

WHAT HOLDS YOU BACK?

Sometimes you can be your own worst enemy, self-sabotaging your dreams and goals with unhelpful habits such as tardiness, arrogance, apathy and so on. This would mean that your goals always elude you, especially if you are not proactively working towards them. Nothing will ever just fall into your lap and an apathetic approach won't get you anywhere. You need to take steps to move your manifestations forward.

Fear is often something that holds people back. The idea of success can be quite a scary prospect, even if you dream of being successful! The reality of your dream might feel uncomfortable. If you have ambitions to start your own business for instance, but the thought of being responsible for your own taxes or hiring an accountant intimidates you, then the chances are that you will

subconsciously sabotage your goal, so as to avoid that level of responsibility. Just like the dark side of the moon is hidden from view, your subconscious fears are often hidden at the back of your mind, but they still have the power to derail your dreams unless you confront them. The following exercise will help you to excavate any fears you might be holding onto in relation to your goal.

BRAINSTORM YOUR FEARS

Take a large sheet of paper and in the centre write a keyword that sums up your main goal. Next add any words that come into your mind, both negative and positive. Try to keep the negative words on the left side of the page and the positive ones on the right, but use up as much space as possible. Once you have all your thoughts on paper, see if you can identify any patterns. If there are more negative words than positive ones, for example, this indicates that your mind-set isn't yet in alignment with your goal, so you would need to work on thinking more positively, in terms of possibility, in order for your dream to manifest. Analyze any negative words to see if they represent variations of the same fear and think about how you can alleviate those fears, or handle the situation in a positive way should the worst happen and your fears come to pass. In this way you can see at a glance whether or not your fears are realistic, and whether your mind-set is supporting your goal or holding you back from achieving it. Once you have this knowledge, then you can begin to take steps to ensure that your mind is your strongest asset in manifestation, rather than your greatest downfall.

YOUR DREAMS WILL WAX AND WANE

It is rare for people to hold only one dream for their entire life. People change and their dreams and goals change with them. What felt like a realistic goal for you at 20 might not be realistic at 60 or 70 years of age. By the same token, an aspiration you once dismissed as nothing more than a pipe-dream might actually manifest later on in life. Accomplishing one goal often leads you onto creating newer, bigger goals – and not all of them will manifest. That's okay because there will be other, more achievable goals which take their place. Your dreams will also change with your circumstances and the roles you take on will alter accordingly. As an example, the job that you were once very happy in may suddenly no longer suit you. It might feel too small, or too stifling because you have outgrown it, or perhaps because you were too big for it in the first place. This is a good thing, as it is a sign of your personal development. When a particular career path, job or relationship is waning for you, try not to fight it. Embrace this change and know that something better will come along to fill the void and your life will begin to wax and grow once more. Reassessing your goals regularly to see if they are still appropriate and achievable will prevent you from wasting valuable time on something that is clearly not working.

LETTING GO OF A DREAM

Letting go of a dream that you have held onto for some time is heart-breaking, but nothing new can come into your life while you are focused on a goal that simply isn't working. In letting go, one of two things will usually happen – either the original goal will suddenly manifest out of nowhere because you stopped holding onto it so tightly, or something better suited to you will come along instead.

It takes courage to let go of an ambition that isn't bearing any fruit. It can feel a lot like failure, yet all you are doing is making space in your life for whatever is *meant* to come to you instead. Be brave and let it go, trusting that the universe has other plans for you. This ritual can help you to come to terms with a defunct ambition, helping you to release it.

A RITUAL TO LET GO OF A DEFUNCT DREAM

You will need a few blessing seeds, also called nigella seeds. On a waning moon, take the blessing seeds outside. Gaze at the waning moon and think about the dream that you are letting go. Consider all the things you did to try and make it manifest. Remember all the disappointments, the tears, the frustration, the rejection, the set-backs, the feeling of banging your head against a wall, of getting nowhere. Try to accept that this goal might not be part of your destiny. When you feel ready, pour a few blessing seeds into your hand and say:

> *I bless the dream I held so dear*
> *I cast it from my heart*
> *I let it go, my path to clear*
> *Disappointment now departs*
> *This goal no longer fills my mind*
> *For it had no fruit to bear*
> *I trust the moon to send in kind*
> *A different joy to share.*

Blow the blessing seeds from your hand out into the night, then turn around and walk away without looking back. Congratulations! You have now cleared the path for something wonderful to come to you instead, so allow yourself to look forward to an unknown blessing.

FINE-TUNE YOUR INNER CIRCLE

The influences that you surround yourself with can either lift you up or drag you down and if it's the latter, then they are also blocking your ability to manifest goals. Remember that like attracts like, so if you are surrounded by negative people they will only bring that negative energy into your life and to your ambitions. This creates a block to your dreams. It's all very well being a member of a popular clique of friends, but if your inner circle is quite a toxic friend group, this can have a very damaging effect on your ability to progress in life and manifest the things you want. Reassessing your relationships is a vital step in manifestation, because you need to be free to follow your own path, rather than modifying your behaviour to suit someone else. Sadly, sometimes it is those who are closest to you who are holding you back or trying to sabotage you in some way.

Toxic people tend to be quite controlling. They want to be at the centre of your life and they try to separate you from more positive influences, which means that they become the sole source of support – or lack thereof. They will try to undermine you in whatever way they can, so if your dream is to go to university, they will try to talk you out of it, or they will disrupt your ability to study by having the TV on loudly in the next room and so on. They might even "accidentally" destroy or damage your work. This is a subtle form of sabotage and a toxic behaviour. If friends or family members are doing their best to keep you down, sneering at your ambitions or planting the seeds of self-doubt with their "concerns", then you need to limit the time you spend with such people and consider keeping your ambitions to yourself.

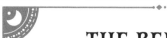

THE BENEFIT OF CUTTING OFF TOXIC PEOPLE

Ending a relationship that has turned toxic is never easy, but no-one is *entitled* to your friendship, especially if they have behaved in a toxic or spiteful manner towards you. Sometimes the gentlest way to extract yourself from such a situation is to allow the friendship to simply fizzle out on its own, by being too busy for gatherings, nights out together and so on. While it can be tough to accept that your friend or family member is having a negative impact on your life and ambitions, you are always entitled to choose who you spend time with – and who you don't!

There are also certain benefits to refining your inner circle in this way, because what frequently happens when you cut away the dead wood of your life is that new shoots start to come through. Ending a toxic relationship often acts as a catalyst, projecting you forwards onto the next level of your life, where exciting new opportunities come along to fill the void. No longer weighed down with someone else's envy, spite, negative attitude or controlling demeanour, you are free to soar to greater heights. Chances are that you will become even *more* successful once you have distanced yourself from people who perhaps didn't actually have your best interests at heart after all. Just don't expect them to like you for it!

AUTHENTIC AMBITION VS A PALE IMITATION

The moon has no light of her own. She has to reflect the light of the sun in order to shine. The same can be true for some people too and there will always be certain individuals who prefer to try and steal someone else's light, rather than taking the time to discover and pursue their own authentic path to success, so you will need to assess whether your goal is a genuine, authentic ambition that comes from within, or an attempt at emulating or usurping the success of someone else.

How do you know the difference? A good indication lies in the timing of your ambition. If your ambition first developed *after* someone you know has already achieved that goal, then the chances are you are imitating that person in order to try and get ahead, level up with them, or even tear them down a few pegs by proving that you can do it too! Likewise, if you prefer to stand back and watch to see if someone else can succeed at something, before you even think about giving it a try yourself, then again, you are acting from a place of imitation, rather than authenticity. This is a classic case of *you go first – I'll hold the rope!* Don't be the one who is holding the rope.

Authentic ambition does not require someone else to lay the groundwork first. An authentic ambition means that you are happy to be the first to blaze that trail yourself and to take all the risks that entails. It means that you are quite prepared to put in the time and effort it takes to succeed, rather than waiting until someone else

has laid the groundwork, and then attempting to follow in their footsteps in an attempt to reap the same results.

This type of toxic imitation is not uncommon and there will always be people who try to hang off the coat-tails of more successful individuals. We see it all the time in celebrity culture, even in schools where pupils try to copy homework from their friends, who they perceive as being more intelligent than themselves. However, there are several reasons why copying and imitation simply don't work in the long run and it is certainly not a path to manifesting lasting success. Here's why.

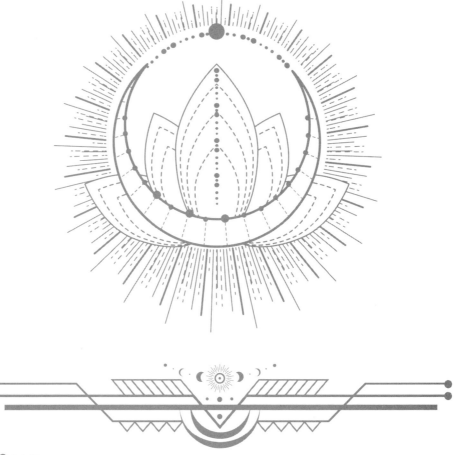

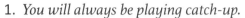

1. *You will always be playing catch-up.*

Whenever you try to emulate someone else, you are immediately setting yourself behind the trend and you will always be struggling to catch up with the success of the people you are emulating. This means that your ideas, goals and designs will be viewed as outdated and lagging behind, which makes success more difficult to achieve.

The flip side, of course, is that the person you are emulating will always have the head start! They already *know* what they are currently working on, or what they plan to do next, but *you* have to wait until they've actually done it before you can put a similar plan into action yourself. This generally means that you will always be working six to 12 months behind the original, possibly even longer. Like it or not, this only adds to the authentic value of the original person's ideas, projects and designs! For example, it takes the high-street clothing chains approximately 12 months to dupe the fashion designs they see on the catwalk, but the very fact that they emulate the big fashion houses at all only increases the perceived value of the original authentic designs, which as a result become more desirable for their authenticity and trend-setting power.

2. *They are already established in their field.*

This goes hand in hand with playing catch-up, because the person you emulate is likely to be a well-established member of their chosen field – otherwise why would you want to emulate them?! They may have been working in this field for considerable time, which means that they have spent years building a good reputation and putting together a network of professional contacts they like to work with,

and who they have successfully collaborated with in the past. By the same token, the professionals in this network are more likely to want to work with their original colleague, rather than taking a chance on an unknown quantity such as yourself, which could be considered too great a risk.

3. *There is no gap in the market for you.*
Being successful in any area involves filling a gap in the market, but when you are emulating someone else's success, then that gap has already been filled by the person or company you are emulating. This effectively means that there isn't really a space for you to fill, especially if you are trying to do exactly the same kind of thing. Why would a movie producer hire a Tom Cruise or Brad Pitt lookalike fresh out of drama school, when they can hire Tom Cruise or Brad Pitt, with all their knowledge, experience and expertise in the film industry, plus an army of adoring fans to sell tickets to? It doesn't make any sense, does it?

The same is true in any field. The market will always prefer to work with the original, rather than an imitation, so you need to find your own alternative market instead, as this means that you have a better chance of finding some kind of gap you can actually fit into. Although this might need to be in a completely different industry, you will actually have a far greater chance of success.

4. *Imitation is no competition!*
When you imitate someone else you might *think* that you are setting yourself up as their direct competition and rival, but let's just unpack that theory. In order to be someone's competition you would first of

all need to be at the same level as them professionally, academically and experientially, because otherwise how can you begin to offer something of the same calibre? It is highly unlikely that a company is going to hire someone who is *less* qualified, with less experience, to do the same job, for the same pay!

In addition, you would need to have the same status and social standing within the industry network, because your social value counts for a lot. There is truth to the saying *it's not what you know, it's who you know*. Most people would rather work with a friend who is part of the industry, who knows how that industry functions, than with a complete stranger who is new to it and still wet behind the ears. So imitating someone who is already established in the field isn't *actually* setting yourself up as competition – it's a silent admission of low self-esteem and a lack of personal direction.

5. *It's a distraction technique.*
Speaking of personal direction, repeatedly trying to emulate the success of someone else is actually a subconscious distraction technique, because it pulls your focus away from discovering your own authentic path to success. While you are busy trying to copy what someone else has done, then you are not working on your own authentic goals and ambitions – you might not even know what they are, because you have been too busy trying to imitate another person's success. Imitation is one of the biggest blocks to manifestation, because you are aiming for something that isn't necessarily meant for you, while at the same time ignoring your true destiny. This in turn leads to feelings of resentment and envy, which can hold you back even further.

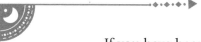

If you have been unsuccessful in emulating another person's success and you have been trying to do so for several years, then take it as a sign that you are on the wrong path! Use the spell from earlier to let go of the dream and begin to embrace your true destiny instead, because that is where your success really lies, but you won't discover it until you stop trying to copy what everyone else is doing.

WHEN SOMEONE IS TRYING TO STEAL YOUR LIGHT

They say that imitation is the sincerest form of flattery. In small doses that may be true, but ongoing imitation can be rather irritating. So what do you do if it's *your* success that people are trying to copy? This can be very frustrating. It's one thing knowing who your genuine competitors are, it's quite another when someone copies everything you do, allowing you to lay the groundwork so that they can try to hang onto your coat-tails and reap the same rewards, without having the relevant qualifications or experience. They are looking for an easy way to the top, because they don't want to make the same effort you have made over the years.

It can be quite infuriating, but take comfort from the fact that if they feel the need to follow someone else, then they probably don't have what it takes to make a success of it, which is why they need to imitate *you* instead. Authentic ambition blazes its own trail. It doesn't play *follow the leader!* That said, you are perfectly entitled to ring-fence and protect your own interests using the following spell.

A WITHERING SPELL TO PROTECT YOUR OWN INTERESTS

A withering spell is a traditional practice witches use to wither away a negative influence or interference in their life. For this spell you will need a small apple, a carving tool such as an athame, garlic powder and a lidded jar big enough to contain the apple. An old candle jar works well.

On the night of the waning moon, carefully carve a keyword or two into the apple skin. So you could carve Shine-Stealer, Usurper or something similar. Hold the apple in your hands close to your chest and repeat this incantation three times to empower it to its purpose.

Those who try to steal my shine
Are now withering away
No longer will you cross the line
No more your game to play
What's mine is mine, I draw the line
I ring-fence my assets true
So go your own way from this day
Find the path that's meant for you.

Place the apple into the jar and sprinkle it liberally with the garlic powder, which is a natural banishing herb. Put the lid on the jar and keep it in a dark place, allowing the apple to wither away. This can take up to six months, until the apple has turned black and mouldy, so keep the spell jar in a garden shed or outside your front door. Once the apple has withered and is black and crumpled, you can throw it away or put it on the compost heap. The spell is complete and the usurper should have moved on to a new goal.

IMITATION VS INSPIRATION

Imitation should not be confused with inspiration. Inspiration is a gift and it is a vital part of any creative life and of manifestation. So what's the difference between the two? We all get inspired by others from time to time. For instance, you might see someone in a great outfit and it inspires you to buy some new clothes or get a new haircut. Or you might hear news of your sister's new job and it inspires you to try for a promotion at work.

Inspiration can come from many places, such as the things you see and hear, the things that are all around you. It hits you in the moment, like a flash in the pan, but rather than setting you on the path to immediate imitation, it is meant to evolve into something that is entirely personal to you.

It is possible to be over-inspired by someone or something, and this is what leads to imitation. If you find yourself copying everything that someone does, or wanting to own and do all the same things as them, then you have been overly inspired and it is time to pull back.

Consider what it is about this person that actually inspired you in the first place – how can you take the essence of that inspiration and re-fashion it to make it entirely your own?

Inspiration is meant to enhance your own pattern and individuality, to help you grow. It's not designed to turn you into a clone of someone else, which is the opposite of personal growth. That's how you stagnate and become fixated on having everything someone else has, rather than building an authentic life of your own. Be inspired by all means, but don't allow yourself to become over-inspired to the point of imitation. After all, you are not the moon – you hold your own light within, so you should have no need to steal the shine off someone else.

CHAPTER SIX
MOON DIVINATIONS

Divination is the art of seeing, commonly known as fortune-telling. It is one of the tricks of the witch's trade and most witches practise some aspect of it. Tarot cards are perhaps the most well-known divination tool, with oracle cards coming in at a close second. If you are interested in card readings, you might find my Moon Magic or Celtic Magic card decks useful. There are lots of other ways to practice divination too. Crystals, water, mirrors and pendulums are all tools used in foretelling the future and we will be looking at some of them in this chapter.

DARK SHADOWS

It is generally accepted that divination is a practice which should be performed after dark. Some witches refuse to do card readings and so on until the sun has set, so it is an aspect of magical living that naturally aligns with the moon. Indeed, there is something very enchanting about setting up a crystal ball or scrying vessel in the dark, with a single candle flame and the moonlight being the only illumination. In the quiet reaches of the night, the unknown becomes known through the shadows reflected in the scrying vessel used.

However, any type of divination is always subject to change, so if you do not like what the crystal ball or whatever is showing you, then you have the option to change your patterns or your approach

to life, in order to effect a different outcome. Nothing is set in stone and the future is always yours to create. Divination shows only what the most likely outcome is, given the current situation. If you alter the situation, then you alter your future too. The shadows of prophecy will shift and change shape based on the decisions you make each day, so divination presents guidance only, rather than a set, unchangeable outcome.

LUNAR DIVINATION TOOLS

In this book we will concentrate on the kind of divination tools which are linked to the moon, so crystals, mirrors, cards and bowls of water. While some crystal balls can be expensive, you do not need to spend a lot of money, for a simple bowl of water can be used in exactly the same way as a crystal ball.

Gazing into a vessel, be it water, mirror or crystal, in order to see images of the past, present or future, is known as scrying. Your scrying vessel should always be clean and dust free, or the water fresh and clear, to give a pure surface on which to scry. With any kind of scrying, visions can come into your mind's eye and this is more common to begin with. With greater practice you might start to see visions in the vessel itself. The first hint that a vision is about to appear in the vessel is when the surface suddenly seems to fill with cloud, or smoke. Maintain your concentration and when the clouds clear, the vision should play out in the vessel. This does take a lot of practice, so persevere.

Crystal Balls

These represent the full moon and are attuned with the Mother aspect of the Triple Goddess. The ball should be a good size without being unwieldy. Traditionally it should fit easily into the palms of both hands, without being too heavy to hold. Ideally it should be placed on a stand, on a table laid with a black or dark-coloured cloth. This gives a shadowy background and ensures there are no gaudy patterns to interfere with the Sight.

Water

This can be a natural body of water such as a loch or lake, but it is usually a bowl of water. Scrying bowls tend to be painted black inside to give a dark surface on which to scry. Water scrying uses the exact same process and techniques as scrying in a crystal ball, but because it is a more dynamic force, you might find that visions come to you more easily. For this reason, it is common practice to begin with water scrying, before moving onto crystal balls and dark mirrors.

Dark Mirrors

A dark mirror, or scrying mirror, is a small mirror with a completely black surface. It could be made from a circle of black obsidian crystal, or it could be homemade, with the sliver removed from a makeup mirror and the back painted black instead. You can even use a TV that is turned off as the black screen provides an instant scrying mirror! Dark scrying mirrors are probably the most difficult to master. They represent the dark moon and are attuned to the Crone. Some of them come as crystal balls too. Again, use the same techniques as with a crystal ball, but be aware that dark mirrors tend to take a bit longer to master.

TIPS FOR A SUCCESSFUL SCRYING SESSION

● *Prepare the room by dimming the lights and lighting a single candle.*

● *Spread a black or dark cloth over a table.*

● *Place your chosen scrying vessel on the table and position yourself so that you can comfortably peer into it.*

● *Breathe slowly and evenly – don't hold your breath.*

● *Repeat a scrying chant such as the ones given opposite.*

● *Concentrate on your question or query.*

● *Gaze into the centre of the vessel, with eyes that are softly focused. Blink when necessary.*

● *Note down any visions you had during your session, which should last no longer than 30 minutes, or you will tire your eyes.*

SCRYING CHANT

It is common practice to begin a scrying session with a special chant. This is a form of spoken intention and helps to set the tone of the session. The chant can be said out loud or whispered under your breath. You can make up your own chant or you can use this one.

Vessel deep shows visions true
Sights unseen betwixt me and you
What is unknown I now shall know
As through this vessel the visions flow
Secrets lost and truth revealed
Past, present and future now unsealed.
So mote it be

ARE MAGIC MIRRORS REAL?

The concept of the magic mirror has been popularized over time by folklore and fairy tales, most notably that of Snow White. There is some truth to the idea that a mirror can reflect visions, for that is what scrying is. It is about learning to see images of the past, present or future within the mirror, or other scrying vessel.

In the Far East, magic mirrors were quite common and their use dates back to approximately the 5th century. These mirrors were usually made of highly polished bronze, with the backs being elaborately decorated. They were highly prized possessions

and would be handed down from one generation to the next, as heirlooms. These mirrors were thought to reflect an unbiased view, offering insights into both good and bad tidings. Once again, this links back to the fairy tale of Snow White and the magic mirrors of myth and legend, which can tell only the truth, regardless of whether the questioner will like it or not. Interestingly, magic mirrors were usually round or oval in shape, linking their power to that of the moon. Modern witches often have a round scrying mirror on their altar, or a round decorative mirror hung in their scared space, to represent the moon and honour her energies.

Scrying mirrors are a more modern version of the Far Eastern magic mirror. They are most commonly made from black obsidian, such as the one said to have been used by John Dee, the famous astrologer to Queen Elizabeth I, which he called his spirit mirror, in reference to the fact that mirrors are said to be portals into the spirit realms and can reflect ghosts, spirits and glimpses into the fairy realm and Otherworld. For this reason, mirrors, scrying mirrors in particular, were often warded with protection magic to prevent any unwelcome guests passing through them as a portal. You will find a warding spell later on in this chapter.

HOW TO MAKE A DARK MIRROR

Moon Phase: Make the mirror during a dark moon.

ITEMS REQUIRED

A round picture frame about the size of a tea plate, matte black paint and a paint brush, or black construction paper or card.

Although you can buy a dark mirror from new age stores and online, you can easily make your own. Take a circular picture frame to represent the moon and carefully remove the glass. Use the paint to cover the back of the glass and let it dry thoroughly. Add a second coat of paint and let this dry too. Alternatively, you could draw around the glass and cut a piece of black card to fit in the frame. Whichever method you choose, reassemble the picture frame with the black paint or card on the inside of the frame. This will keep the paint from scratching off or the card from ripping. You now have a dark mirror for your scrying sessions. Keep it on your lunar altar and use it for divination.

PROTECTION MAGIC TO WARD A DARK MIRROR

To make sure that your scrying vessel is safe to use, you will need to protect it with a warding spell. First of all, cleanse the mirror by passing incense smoke all around it. You can use a smudge stick, an incense stick, or some of the Wish Fulfilment incense from the last chapter. Next, sprinkle the mirror with a little sea salt, which acts as a blessing. Finally, ward the mirror by dipping your finger into some lunar oil and tracing a pentagram, or five-pointed star, on the back of the mirror as you say the following words of power:

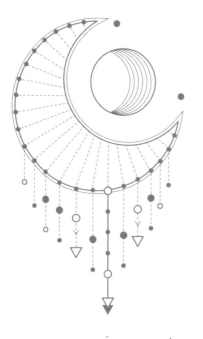

No ill or bane this path shall seek
As visions true, the Scryer seeks
Visions come for highest good
I ward this mirror with a protective hood
So mote it be.

DEVELOPING YOUR SECOND SIGHT

Any type of divination can take time to master because it depends on your own personal level of psychic ability, or second sight, as it is sometimes known. Many people believe that you must be born with second sight, that it is a gift only a few people are blessed with. In fact, it is part of the survival instinct and we all have it within us. Your intuition is one of your most valuable assets. It is that part of you that instinctively has a good or bad feeling about a stranger you hardly know, or that prompts you to find an alternative route to work, only to discover later that there was heavy traffic or a road accident on your usual route.

We often credit animals with having great instincts, but the human instinct is no less finely tuned. Your intuition, or second sight, is a natural human ability. It works like a muscle, so the more you use it, the more it develops over time. Start to listen to your instincts more frequently. Pay attention to what they are trying to tell you and act upon this instinct. If you do, you will find that your insights from divination become much more profound. Use the following ritual to signal to your intuition that you are ready to listen, ready to *see* that which is otherwise unseen.

LUNAR CHARM FOR SECOND SIGHT

As you settle down to perform your divination practices, first of all light a white candle and say, *I work in the light of all lights.* Next, close your eyes and breathe deeply three times. Picture the moon in your mind and now say:

> *Lunar Lady, Mother of dark and light*
> *Open my mind's eye this night*
> *As I see a dream within a dream*
> *Reveal to me the realms of Unseen*
> *Instincts strong and visions true*
> *I welcome the Sight, as I learn from you.*

When you feel ready, open your eyes and begin to scry or deal the cards. Enjoy your gift of second sight. Divination should not feel scary. You are simply tapping into your intuition in a magical way, and intuition is a natural gift.

LUNAR STONES FOR DIVINATION

Moon Phase: Put this divination tool together on the night of the full moon.

ITEMS REQUIRED
A small pouch, lavender oil, tumble stones of the following crystals – clear quartz, snowy quartz, red jasper, moonstone, hematite.

First sprinkle the pouch, both inside and out, with a few drops of lavender oil. This will act as a cleansing agent to keep your crystals pure and free of negative energy. Each crystal represents a phase of the lunar cycle. Place them into the pouch and give them a shake. When you want to use them, shake the pouch three times as you ask your question, then draw out a single lunar crystal. Use the guide to interpret the answer to your question.

Clear Quartz – This represents the new moon, meaning new beginnings are under way but as yet unseen. The shoots are about to burst through, but on the surface everything looks dead and fallow. Have faith that things are being put into place for your highest good. You are surrounded by Maiden energy.

Snowy Quartz – This represents the waxing moon, meaning a time of fresh starts and planning is underway. Good things are coming to you and you are working hard to achieve your goals. You are surrounded by positive energy.

Red Jasper – This represents the full moon and the blood of the mother goddess. This is a vibrant time and you are reaping the rewards of your labour, however, it is not without difficulty or sacrifice. The end result will be worth the pain. You are surrounded by Mother energy.

Moonstone – This represents the waning moon, meaning that the hard work is done and a brief time of respite is to come. The cloudy aspect of this crystal means that you might not be able to see your way ahead right now, but trust that all will be well, given time.

Hematite – This represents the dark moon, meaning that you need to rest and recharge in preparation for the next cycle of growth and activity. Something may have been stripped from your life and you need to grieve the loss, or you may be experiencing a period of fatigue. Rest, recharge and recuperate at this time. New seeds are being sown in the darkness. You are surrounded by Crone energy.

SMOKE ON, GO!

Moon Phase: This is a good ritual for a waning or dark moon.

ITEMS REQUIRED
A cauldron or heatproof bowl, sand, charcoal blocks, a lighter, dried herbs such as mugwort, white sage, basil and mint are good ones to use.

Smoke scrying is less well known than crystal or water scrying, but it can be very relaxing and beneficial for mental health. Make sure that you are outdoors or in a well-ventilated room, away from any smoke detectors.

Fill the cauldron or bowl with sand to absorb the heat safely, then light a charcoal block and place it in the centre of the bowl. Next add the dried herbs to the charcoal block, a pinch at a time so that they burn slowly. The smoke will rise quite quickly, forming patterns in the air. Watch as these patterns unfold, making special note of any images you see such as hearts, arrows and other symbols. Use your intuition to interpret what these images mean for you. If the smoke is bringing the image towards you, that is a sign that it is coming your way, but if the smoke carries it away from you, then it is not meant to be, or will not happen for a long while. If the image travels straight up, the timing is as yet unclear. If the charcoal block goes out or the herbs don't burn, then it is not meant to be.

You can enhance your smoke scrying sessions by backlighting the smoke with a coloured light, such as a pink-salt lamp. This gives the smoke added definition and makes it easier to scry out images and patterns.

MOTHER OF DARK AND LIGHT

Moon Phase: Make this stone at the time of the full moon.

ITEMS REQUIRED
A round pebble or stone, black paint, white paint and two paint brushes, clear varnish.

As you have seen throughout this book, the moon and the mother goddess she represents is both light and dark, waxing and waning, Mother and Crone. We can tap into both these energies in divination.

Divination need not be complicated and sometimes all you need is a simple yes or no answer to a simple question. This is known as *binary divination.* The most popular binary divination tool is the pendulum, but you can also make a simple *binary stone* to achieve the same results. First find a pebble on the beach or the riverside. It should be roundish to represent the moon and it should feel nice in your hand. Take it home with you and paint one side white to represent the answer *Yes.* Allow the paint to dry, then turn the stone over and paint the other side black to represent the answer *No.* Wait for the paint to dry before varnishing the entire stone to protect the paint. To use the stone, ask a simple binary question, then toss the stone in the air like you would a coin and see which side faces up when it lands. If the white side is facing upwards the answer to your question is yes, but if the black side is facing up the answer is no.

CARTOMANCY

Cartomancy is the art of using cards for insight, clarity and foresight – commonly known as fortune-telling or prophecy. As soon as playing cards were introduced in the 14th century, people began to interpret them to mean certain things, for instance, the King or Queen of Hearts represented a new love interest, while the Jack of Hearts was someone to avoid! Likewise, the Ace of Spades was said to foretell a death in the family.

Each card held its own meaning, each suit represented something different. Hearts meant love and relationships, Clubs creativity and travel, Spades meant misfortune, warnings or conflict, while Diamonds heralded wealth and business ventures. The suits also corresponded to the four most common career paths of the Middle Ages, with the Hearts signifying the church, Spades the military, Clubs farming and agriculture and Diamonds merchants and business.

Over time, new card decks were introduced specifically for the purpose of divination, such as the tarot deck. These decks have been both revered and feared at various points in history. There was a time when to be found in possession of a tarot deck would most likely lead to a charge of witchcraft and possible hanging. However, these days we are safe to practise whatever kind of divination we choose, including cartomancy. If you want to use cards in your lunar divinations, then follow these simple tips to get the most out of your readings:

☾ Wait until sunset before performing a reading.

☾ Lay your cards on a plain, dark cloth so that the images are vibrant.

☾ Read your cards by candlelight or moonlight if possible.

☾ Cast your cards on the night of the full moon for the most prophetic results.

☾ Cleanse your cards with smoke on a waning moon.

☾ Bless your cards on a new or full moon by letting them sit in moonlight overnight.

☾ Try not to let anyone else handle your oracle cards – they should soak up your energy alone.

☾ Say a card blessing just before a reading, such as the one on page 164.

THE FOOL

THE HIGH PRIESTESS

THE LOVERS

ORACLE CARD BLESSING CHARM

As you shuffle the deck, repeat the following charm three times, then immediately deal the cards into your preferred spread. This will help to ensure the most accurate readings and an insightful session.

Card by card let the future unfold
Image by image a story is told
A pattern plays within this spread
For helpful insight, nothing to dread
For as the moon doth wax and wane
A question is posed, an answer is gained
Blessed be.

CHAPTER SEVEN
SHADOW CRAFT

Moon magic isn't only about spell craft and astrological signs and symbols. It is also about the shadow craft in the darker reaches of the mind, the conscious and the unconscious and how they work together to create your reality. The light of the moon is mesmeric and meditative, sometimes full and bright, sometimes hidden by cloud, but always powerful. In the same way, the unconscious mind is always working away, although we are generally unaware of it. Programming the unconscious mind is a way of ensuring that your inner landscape remains positive and doesn't sabotage your chances of success. Likewise, you can tap into your unconscious mind, also known as the higher self, for guidance and self-support.

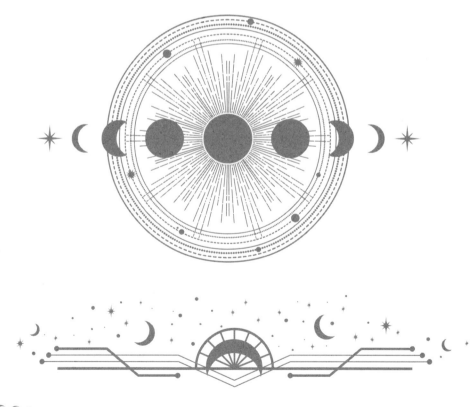

FINDING QUIET AMID CHAOS

The world can seem like quite a chaotic place at times and it can be difficult to keep that chaos from impacting your life and your mental well-being. However, being able to find a sense of calm and quiet amid this chaos is essential if you are to maintain peace of mind. Chaos, panic, fear and anxiety are all infectious, so it is vital that you learn to create your own boundary of mental peace and quiet. Think of the poem *If* by Rudyard Kipling and learn to "keep your head when all about are losing theirs and blaming it on you"!

Recognizing the first stirrings of chaos is often half the battle. If you know that your workplace is stretched to breaking point at certain times, or you know that certain people carry drama with them like a torch of doom, then you can prepare yourself for the madness in advance. Sometimes, though, chaos comes out of the blue. Accidents, illnesses and bereavements can all take us by surprise, bringing a certain amount of chaos with them, which is unavoidable. Try using this magical technique to find a space of calm and quiet when your environment turns frenzied.

MOONLIGHT SHIELD VISUALIZATION

Go to a quiet place and close your eyes. Breathe deeply three or four times. This will help to calm your nerves. Now in your mind's eye, visualize the full moon high in the sky, shining her light down on you. Feel the silvery rays on your skin and bathe in this imaginary light. In this way you are tapping into the lunar energies, even if its midday, through the power of visualization. Next imagine that the lunar rays form a shield of light all around you, sealing you in and keeping any negative chaos or drama at bay. Within this shield you are calm and peaceful, capable and strong. Once you can see yourself surrounded by a magical shield of moonlight, open your eyes, take three more deep breaths and go back out into the fray, knowing that you can handle the chaos by presenting the light of peace and calm.

SCHEDULE PSYCHIC QUIET TIME

Lunar energies are quiet by nature. While the sun can be brash and obnoxious, the moon is gentle and subtle. The night-time energies are ones which we often ignore, preferring the company of the family sitting around the TV on a dark night to that of the stars and moon, but communing with the nightscape is a great way to enhance your psychic abilities and your natural instincts.

There is something magical about being awake when most people are fast asleep and the wee small hours of the night hold enchantment within them. The dark night encompasses the magical hours of storytelling – the witching hour of midnight, the devil's hour of 3am and the fairy hours of dusk and dawn. Try to schedule some psychic quiet time around these hours, perhaps going for a walk at dusk or dawn, or conducting a midnight scrying session or card reading. Perhaps you could do some star gazing during the devil's hour, in the safety of your garden or a friend's. Providing you are sensible and do not put yourself at risk, there is no reason why you cannot enjoy the nocturnal hours to your witchy heart's content. Enjoy the magic of the nightscape and commune with the moon.

THE WITCHING HOUR

The stroke of midnight is a liminal space between the end of one day and the start of the next. As such it is said to be infused with its own kind of magic. This magic is generally regarded as being positive and enchanting in nature. It heralds the beginning of the witching hour, which traditionally lasts until around 2am. It has often been linked to witches, fairies, prophetic dreams and visions. The witching hour is said to be an especially auspicious time for magic and spell casting, so many modern witches use this time to add power to special rituals. Here are some tips for how you can make the most of this magical time of night.

☾ Take a ritual bath, steeped in Epsom, Dead Sea or Himalayan salts.

☾ Perform a midnight divination.

☾ Try astral projection exercises.

☾ Write in your moon journal.

☾ Work a dream incubation spell.

☾ Cast a spell or ritual attuned with the moon phase.

☾ Enjoy a midnight picnic with friends in a safe place, such as your garden.

☾ Cleanse your crystals and magical tools.

☾ Do gentle bedtime yoga or some stretching exercises.

☾ Meditate – you can use one of the guided meditations in this book or something else.

THE DEVIL'S HOUR

The devil's hour is said to be around 3am. However, the term can also refer to any time after the midnight witching hour has passed and before the dawn chorus begins, so usually between 2am and 4am. In folklore, this is the time when hauntings are said to occur and ghostly spirits are believed to walk abroad at night. The devil's hour indicates a time when spooky things are more likely to happen. It is also a time when only those people who are working a nightshift (or those who are up to no good!) are out and about, as the rest of the world sleeps comfortably in their beds.

Most people have had the experience of waking suddenly in the middle of the night. The world is dark and quiet and you might wonder what it was that woke you from your slumber. This sudden jolt from sleep can mean that you wake in a panic, with your heart racing and your body drenched in a night sweat, especially if you were having a bad dream.

Waking up, into the silence that accompanies the darkest part of the night, can be quite unnerving. Everything is quiet; any noise you hear outside is automatically suspicious and any creaks coming from inside the house are easily attributed to ghostly goings-on. It's a spooky time of night and your imagination does its best to fill in the gaps, offering possible explanations of why you woke up in the first place – burglars, wildlife, ghosts?

The truth is that it is highly unlikely to be either ghosts or intruders that woke you, but something more mundane, such as an addiction, a drop in body temperature or a dip in your blood-sugar levels. If you are a smoker, for example, often it is the body's craving for nicotine that wakes you in the night and chances are you can fall back to sleep again after feeding the craving with a few puffs of a cigarette. For non-smokers, the chill that accompanies a deep sleep, during which your body temperature drops, can be enough to bring you round temporarily, as you reach for an extra blanket or snuggle deeper under the covers. What if you wake up filled with dread, depression and dark thoughts? Well, scientists believe that this is most likely to be caused by a temporary drop in your blood sugar, which can cause low mood and melancholia. The remedy? Raise your sugar levels slightly by eating something sweet, such as a biscuit, a small piece of fruit or a small square of chocolate and you should find that you can drop off to sleep again more easily.

MOONSTRUCK MELANCHOLIA

Sometimes the moon itself has a part to play in nocturnal low moods and night-time depression, because it helps the body to provide vitamin D. Although we often associate this vitamin with sunlight, because the moon *reflects* the sun's light, it too can boost your vitamin D levels. Sleeping with the blinds open can help to facilitate this. However, when the moon is waning or dark, it provides less light, meaning that your body converts less vitamin D as you sleep. This reduction in moonlight can have a similar affect to Seasonal Affective Disorder, which is where some people experience low mood during the darker months of autumn and winter, due to the lack of natural light.

During the latter half of the lunar cycle, when the moon wanes towards its darkest phase, you may experience an increase in night-time depression and low mood in the evenings. This is a perfectly natural reaction to the lack of moonlight and it's nothing to worry about. Usually it doesn't require any kind of medical intervention, as your mood will begin to lift again as the moon waxes towards full. It can, however, play havoc with your sleep patterns and circadian rhythm, leaving you over-tired, miserable and irritable. If this type of moon melancholia is something that you suffer from, then a simple remedy would be to take a vitamin D supplement during the time of the waning moon. You could also try eating more foods that are naturally rich in vitamin D, such as oily fish, eggs and red meat, during this phase of the lunar cycle. Also, try to get outside more during the day and make the most of the natural light that is available.

MOON BLUES

Night-time depression is a real issue for some people. They might feel okay during the day when they are busy and productive, but as soon as their head touches the pillow, intrusive thoughts kick in, leading to low mood, depression, bad dreams and sleepless nights. Sometimes it can seem as if all your worries are resting upon the pillow, just waiting to invade your mind and keep you awake at night.

Anyone can be affected by the moon blues, not just people who have a medical history of depression. This kind of low mood usually begins in the evening, as you wind down for the night. It creeps up on you bit by bit, until you feel sad and tearful by the time you go to bed. It is usually triggered by the quietness of the night, when you are not being distracted by screens or family responsibilities and there is nothing between you and your worries.

Pondering on the events of the day, worrying about the following day, mental stress, poor health, having too many responsibilities, financial anxiety and so on can all trigger a bout of night-time depression.

We see this a lot in children who, as the evening wears on, with bedtime approaching, start to think about school the next day, gradually becoming quieter, less playful, more withdrawn, possibly even tearful. This is a classic sign that something is playing on their mind and all is not well. The same is true for adults too, but we frequently dismiss the symptoms.

So what can you do if you, or someone you know, is experiencing night-time depression? First of all, try to make the experience of winding down for the night as pleasurable as possible. Having a night-time routine can be very comforting and reassuring, particularly if you are going through a difficult time or you have a stressful job. Play soft music that you only listen to at night, or make a playlist you can fall asleep to. Invest in a white-noise machine and listen to the soothing sounds of the sea, rainfall or crickets and frogs as you drop off to sleep. These are simple techniques that help to fill your mind with sound, rather than with worry or anxiety and so they help to keep troublesome thoughts at bay.

Try to make it a rule that you never go to bed without addressing your worries in some way first, whether that means talking them through with a loved one or writing them down in a moon journal. Do what you can to get your concerns out in the open, so that they have less power to ambush you from your pillow in the middle of the night!

THE WORRY POPPET

Worry dolls and poppets have been in use for centuries, originating in South America and becoming a popular tool of esoteric therapy. Traditionally made from scraps of fabric, beads, pegs, pipe cleaners and so on, worry dolls are very easy to make at home. The traditional European alternative is of course the humble bedtime teddy bear, which serves the same purpose, giving children somewhere to place their worries before they go to sleep, but this is a technique that adults can benefit from too. First decide what kind of poppet you want to use as your worry doll. This could be a handmade poppet, or a much-loved doll or teddy from childhood. Once you have the doll, cleanse it by sprinkling it with a solution of salt water, then hold it and empower it to its purpose with these words or something similar:

Poppet of worry and of woe
Take my fears, I let them go
Hold the worries I give to you
Transform them into a dream come true
Keep my worries till break of day
Chasing fear right away

To use the poppet, simply tell it your fears, worries and concerns before you go to sleep each night and then repeat the charm above.

MEDITATION

Meditation is another great way to attune with the inner reaches of the mind and that which is hidden. Just like the moon, your higher self is always there, but you may not always listen to its wisdom, so meditating gives your higher self a chance to communicate with your conscious mind. In meditation you are inviting your subconscious to take centre stage for a time, to offer advice, encouragement and guidance. It has many benefits, both mentally and physically. Spending time in meditation can help you to relax, it reduces levels of stress and anxiety, and it can alleviate feelings of irritability or restlessness. Meditation is also good for increasing your sense of self-awareness and emotional intelligence, plus it has the added benefit of developing your patience and a sense of control over your emotions.

Building a meditative exercise into your magical practice is a fantastic way to learn about visions, pre-cognition and prophecy, dream worlds and other realms, the meaning of signs and symbols etc. In addition, it helps to develop your visualization skills, and in turn your ability to envision and manifest a better future for yourself, so there are really no reasons not to give it a try! Guided meditations, such as the one below, are often the best to begin with because, as the name suggests, they take you on a mental journey, guiding you through an imaginary realm before bringing you back to the current moment in time. A guided mediation, also known as a path-working, is a bit like mindfulness but with storytelling attached! Try the path-working below and see what it brings up for you.

PERSEPHONE'S LABYRINTH OF THE DARK MOTH

For this guided meditation it is useful to have someone read it out loud to you, or alternatively, you can record it in advance so that you can play it back whenever you want to. Lie down in a comfortable position and close your eyes. Breathe deeply for a while, until you start to feel nicely relaxed, then proceed to visualize the guided meditation below.

You find yourself standing on a forest path. The night air is bracing and chill. The moon above is bright and full, lighting your way. You set off walking through the woods. In the distance you hear a soft voice whispering your name. It sounds as if the dry autumn leaves are calling out to you. You follow the path through the woods until you come to a moss-covered cave.

A woman stands at the mouth of the cave, wearing a flowing gown in the dark colours of autumn: mulberry, grey, bronze and deep purple. A lacy network of cobwebs is draped over the fabric, bejewelled with dewdrops which glimmer in the moonlight and a sweeping train falls from the gown, made up of dry autumn leaves. Her hair falls in a dark curtain, almost to her knees and her dark eyes have a glint of amber gold within them. She is Persephone, Lady of the Underworld, Mistress of Shadows and Spirits. She beckons you to follow her and you walk behind her down a steep path, tangled with tree roots and overhung with boughs of fir trees, until you find yourself in a grove of trees and at the beginning of a labyrinth.

"Welcome to my dark labyrinth, Shadow Weaver. Shall we venture into its centre to see who awaits?" You nod your head and follow Persephone as she leads you along the winding path of the labyrinth. As she walks, she begins to chant and you join in with her song.

"Ever circling, ever turning, take me to the centre;
Ever constant, every changing, moving to the centre."

After a time, you find yourself in the very centre of the labyrinth, where a stone pillar supports a beautiful ornate lantern. Persephone moves to the lantern, lights the candle within and says:

"At the centre of all things is the light of all lights, the light of
Spirit and the light of hope, reflecting the promise of the moon
above."

The ornate knotwork of the lantern casts dancing shadows
around the labyrinth. The fir trees sway in the breeze, seeming
to dance in the candlelight. A tiny black moth flies out of the
darkness to the light of the lantern. Again and again the little
moth flies against the lantern and you watch in fascination until,
in a single quick movement, Persephone reaches out and gently
catches the moth. It sits peacefully in her hand and you take a
closer look at its beautiful dark markings.

"Light any spark in the dark and the moth will come, for he is eternally drawn to the deeper darkness beyond the flame. As he struggles to reach the shadow-side of candlelight, he exerts himself, constantly striving to reach his dark goal, until he is his own undoing. For of course, it is an illusion and the moth will never attain the deeper darkness, except in his own demise.

"Human nature is very similar. You have a tendency to believe that circumstances are somewhat blacker and darker than they really are, so you do not see the light. You forget to respect its heat and warmth, so you become burned by sorrow. Remember that in the darkest of times, the light is always there, if you only look for it." Persephone blows gently on the moth and it flies away into the night, unscathed by its brush with fire.
"Go now, Shadow Weaver, and walk the labyrinth back to your own realm." You leave Persephone in the middle of the labyrinth and take the circling path back out into the woods. Eventually you see the cave and the path back to the world of consciousness.

When you feel ready, open your eyes and become aware of your surroundings. Write down your mediation experiences, and how Persephone's words have resonated with you, in your moon journal, then go about your day.

MOON JOURNAL

If you haven't started a moon journal yet, then I urge you to do so. Traditionally magical journals are handwritten, but you can start a digital one if you prefer, or add a moon magic section to your current Book of Shadows if you have one. Use the moon journal to keep track of your meditations, spells, rituals, manifestations and so on. It is also wise to make a note of how the moon affects your moods and behaviours as she moves through her cycle. Do you feel most powerful at the full moon during the time of the Mother, or during a waning or dark moon during the time of the Crone? How does a new moon make you feel – optimistic, nervous, restless? Keeping a moon journal will reinforce your connection to lunar energies and you can record your most successful rituals, so that you can repeat the patterns that work for you. Remember that all magic is a personal journey and your path is a unique one which only you are destined to tread. Here are some tips for what to add to your moon journal:

☾ Favourite crystals and the lunar energies they work best with;

☾ The moon cycle and how it reflects in your moods;

☾ Herbs and night flowering blooms you can use in lunar spells;

☾ Your dreams and how they alter throughout the moon's phases;

☾ Your patterns of concentration – does the moon have an impact?;

☾ Favourite spells and rituals for attuning with the moon;

☾ Lunar deities and their attributes;

☾ Lunar totems you would like to work with in ritual;

☾ Different moon names from different cultures, or devise your own;

☾ Esbat rituals and traditions.

CHAPTER EIGHT
DARK NIGHTS OF DREAMING

our dreams are far more than somnambulistic rambles through night-time realms of wonder and imagination. They are a way to process life events, work through your emotions, face fears and even find solutions to problems. Everyone dreams. It is a natural part of your nightly sleeping pattern. However, you may not always remember your dreams. Sometimes they fade almost as soon as you have opened your eyes, while at other times the dream is so vivid it stays with you for the rest of the day.

Many people believe that the moon has a profound effect on their dreams and their sleeping patterns in general. It is not uncommon to have a more restless night and more vivid dreams during a full moon, for instance. This could be because the night sky is much brighter, making a deep, dreamless sleep more difficult.

You might also see the moon in your dreams as well, with different lunar phases thought to signify different things. Dreaming of a new moon could mean that a fresh challenge is on the way, while a full moon denotes success. Dreaming of a waning or dark moon, or the moon hidden by mist or cloud, is thought to represent something which is hidden or repressed weighing on your mind. Dreaming is a magical experience in its own right. In your dreams you can fly, have superpowers, win the lotto or meet your idols. There are no limits. A whole world of possibility is open to you as you slumber. You will spend approximately one third of your life asleep, so with all this going on, it makes sense

to try and harness such power, or at the very least, understand it a little better.

AND SO TO BED . . .

Creating a peaceful night-time routine is the first step in harnessing your nocturnal visions. You need to feel safe, warm and comfortable in order to have a good night's sleep. You should also be as relaxed as possible and for this purpose, lavender is your best friend. Begin your night routine with a lavender-scented bath or shower. There are hundreds of lavender-based bath and body products on the market for all budgets, so you should be able to find something you like. Next open the bedroom window slightly to allow the night air to circulate and draw the blinds if you wish, or leave them open to the moon's rays.

Ensure that your bed is as comfy as you can make it, without it being stifling. The idea is to cocoon yourself in soft nightwear and bedclothes. Scent your bedding with a lavender pillow spray or a few drops of lavender oil. You could also burn a lavender-scented candle for half an hour before you turn out the light and go to sleep. Grab a relaxing drink such as hot chocolate or a special cup of night-time tea, and curl up under the duvet with a good book. Sip your tea and read until you feel drowsy, then blow out the candles, turn off the lights and sleep, perchance to dream.

THE PSYCHOLOGY OF SLEEPING POSITIONS

Your preferred sleeping position says a lot about your state of mind and psychologists have come up with interesting interpretations for each posture. While we move through many positions each night, the one that you habitually adopt is your natural preference.

☾ *Foetal* – curled up, with knees brought up to the chest and arms tucked in. This is the position of the babe in the womb and is the most common sleeping position. Both children and adults adopt this pose. It indicates a fairly relaxed person, though it can also relate to shyness and timidity. Interestingly it is often the position adopted by someone who is going through a trauma of some kind, reflecting their inner feelings of insecurity and the need to curl up and protect themselves. People often adopt this position when they need to have a good cry.

☾ *Log* – sleeping on the side, legs and arms straight down. This denotes a fairly balanced individual, one who is open to others and quite sociable. However, there is also a total lack of defence in this position which means that it can be easy to take advantage of this person.

☾ *Yearning* – another side position, but this time the sleeper might have one leg slightly bent as if stepping forward. Also the arms tend to be reaching out away from the body, as if trying

to hold onto something. This is perhaps the most vulnerable of the poses, indicating a fragile personality who has in all likelihood experienced trauma of some kind. The outstretched arms could just as easily be used for defence, though, and this denotes a lack of trust in others and a willingness to stand up for themselves.

☾ *Soldier* – flat on the back, legs slightly apart, arms relaxed by the side. This is the pose of complete confidence! This *sunbathing* position indicates someone with a strong sense of self, one who is comfortable being the centre of attention. They know who they are and what they want from life and they are ready to go out and get it. However, the soldier is always on high alert and this individual might have trouble truly relaxing and letting go of control.

☾ *Freefall* – flat on the stomach, face turned to one side, arms bent at the elbows with the hands raised. This is the position of someone who is completely closed off from others. It is a pose of self-protection, as all the vital organs are tucked in close to the mattress and the heart is turned away, as the sleeper presents their back to the room. This denotes someone who is suspicious and who does not trust or open up to other people very easily.

☾ *Starfish* – flat on the back, arms and legs spread wide, reaching towards the four corners of the mattress and taking up as much space as possible. This denotes someone who is always ready to help other people. They are ready to leap into action at a moment's notice and enjoy being of service to others, yet it can lead to a martyr mind-set or overextending oneself if not carefully monitored.

TYPES OF DREAMS

There are various types of dreams, from those that recur over and over again to the terror of the nightmare. Most of us experience a wide variety of dreams, often experiencing two or three types within the same night. Keeping a record can help you to identify the kind of dreams you have and how the moon might be affecting them. Lots of people like to write down their dreams as soon as they wake up, keeping a notepad and pen by the bed for this purpose. You could also make a voice note on your phone.

Whatever way you choose to record your dreams it is highly likely that they will fall into one of the following categories.

☾ *Precognitive Dreams* – Usually these are visions of something which has yet to happen, also known as annunciation dreams. You might dream that you have a baby then discover that you are pregnant, or you might dream that you get your ideal job etc.

☾ *Lucid Dreams* – This is when you have the sudden realization within the dream that you are in fact dreaming and it is not real. Often people wake up shortly after becoming lucid in their dreams, but if you can manage to remain asleep, sometimes you can take control of the dream and direct it like a movie. This takes practice though.

☾ *Incubated Dreams* – This is when you have asked for a very specific dream to come to you, perhaps for guidance or answers to a problem.

☾ *Recurring Dreams* – dreaming of the same thing over and over again. Pay special attention to these dreams as they are usually a message from your higher self. Once you act upon the message the dreams will stop.

☾ *Visitation Dreams* – dreaming of the dead. These dreams often happen on special anniversaries such as birthdays or the anniversary of the death. They bring comfort and guidance and should not be discounted as imagination. Waking up can be tough though, as the loss is felt once more.

☾ *Nightmares* – Also known as night terrors, these dreams urge us to face our fears. Common nightmares which we all have include being chased or hunted, falling from a great height, being naked in public, being laughed at on stage, crashing a car or plane, drowning, and failing some kind of exam or test.

DREAMING OF A PAST LIFE

In addition to the types of dreams above, you might experience dreams that show a life you lived before, in a different incarnation. In these

past-life dreams you are likely to have a completely different appearance which becomes apparent only when you do something mundane in the dream, such as look in a mirror or brush out your hair. Such dreams might be accompanied by a feeling of déjà vu or a sense of knowing that you are seeing visions of the past. People might call you by a different name, or you will be surrounded by faces you don't know but feel connected to. Often you and those around you will be wearing clothes from a different time period. It is also not unusual in these dreams to see how you died. It might feel brutal at the time, but check your birthmarks when you wake up, as these are said to be leftover traumatic injuries from past lives. Do you have a birthmark that matches with an injury or death blow from the past-life dream? If so, it could be your soul's way of reminding you that you have many lifetimes of experience and wisdom to draw upon.

DREAMWEAVER

Dream incubation is the practice of requesting that a particular type of dream come to you within the next few nights. There are many reasons why you might decide to do this. It could be that you wish to connect with your ancestors or a deceased loved one via a visitation dream, or you want to experience a past-life dream or a lucid dream that you can control. Whatever your reasons, sleeping on an issue can be hugely beneficial, so try this ritual and see what turns up in the night, as you allow your dreams to tell you a bedtime story.

How to Incubate a Dream

To begin, think about the kind of dream you want to have and write it down on a piece of paper. You might put something like *I wish to meet my deceased grandmother in dreams because I miss talking to her.* Once you have the intention of the dream written down, add a drop of lavender essential oil to the paper, then fold it and place it within your pillow case. Sprinkle a drop or two of the oil onto the pillow case, lie down and relax. Whisper what you want to dream about into your pillow as you fall asleep. This might not work immediately, but within the next seven nights, the dream you requested should manifest itself. Just be sure to write it down when you wake up!

RIDING THE NIGHTMARE

Nightmares or night terrors are a type of intrusive thought. These disturbing visions can have an adverse effect on your mental, emotional and physical health, especially if they happen frequently. In order to begin taming the night mare we need to understand where she comes from.

In folklore, the "night mare" was a spirit horse often associated with the equine goddesses Epona or Rhiannon, as well as the Kelpie of Celtic legend. The kelpie was a fairy horse that would graze by the side of a loch, waiting for an unsuspecting human to come along. Initially it would be friendly, allowing itself to be petted, but as soon as it was mounted or bridled, the kelpie was said to gallop back into the depths of the loch, drowning its rider in the process. Interestingly, the element of water is linked to dreams, intuition and emotion, so it makes sense that the kelpie, with its lethal dash into the water, is a version of the night mare.

Perhaps the most famous night mare of all is the one depicted in Henry Fuseli's 1781 painting *The Nightmare*, which shows a fearsome horse's head peeking thorough the bedcurtains at a sleeping woman. Accompanying the horse in his observation of the sleeper is a small demon squatting on her chest. This relates to the sensation of feeling a weight pressing down on the chest that some people experience during a bad dream. Often this sensation is caused by stress, indigestion or respiratory issues, yet the 18th-century notion that it was caused by the presence of a demon has become a common, if rather romantic, aspect of dream lore.

Another indication of the night mare's presence in your dreams is that of sleep paralysis, which is when your mind wakes up moments

before your body receives the message that it is time to awaken. This effectively means that although you are semi-conscious, you can't move your body for a few seconds after waking, leading to feelings of panic until the paralysis passes and you can move again. People also report sensing a presence in the room with them when they experience sleep paralysis, which further increases their unease and terror. This can happen as you transition from waking to sleeping and vice versa.

Although sleep paralysis happens when you are semi-conscious, either as you begin to drop off to sleep or when you wake up, it is still considered to be a form of night terror and a sleep disorder. However, it is a natural phenomenon, because it is caused by the body being programmed to lie still when in a deep sleep so as to protect itself from injury.

Back in Henry Fuseli's time, though, none of this would have been common knowledge and sleep disorders would have been explained by tales of demons and phantom horses sent in the night to spirit you away as you slept. Thus the "night mare" was created.

SHADES, SHADOWS AND DARK-MAN DREAMS

Sensing a presence in the bedroom during your sleep is often the most disturbing sleep disorder you can ever experience, especially when you open your eyes and see a shadowy figure standing in the corner, or worse, leaning over you as you slumber! Sleepers sometimes experience the sensation of having the breath sucked out of them by these shades and they may wake up coughing or gasping for breath. Such nocturnal visions can be quite terrifying, especially when they bleed into the first waking moments of reality, but they are also fairly common. People from all over the world, from all different cultures have reported having such dreams, so where do these visions and hallucinations come from?

The figures we see in our dreams usually relate to people we know, or those we wish we knew. Dreaming of a famous singer or actor would be a typical wish-fulfilment dream, while dreaming of your old teacher might indicate that you are feeling more studious or have recently accomplished something that you are proud of.

Night-time visits from shades and shadowy figures however, are much less congenial and each one is slightly different in nature. A shade is usually a coalescence of dark energy and may appear as an insubstantial shadow with no defined shape. If this kind of apparition is disturbing your sleep, then clear away the dark energy by cleansing your bedroom with incense or a smudge stick. Do this during a waning moon, moving in an anti-clockwise direction, to draw the dark energy away from you.

A shadowy figure is rather more sinister and usually has the appearance of a tall man, hence why these nightmares are sometimes referred to as *dark-man dreams*. Often this figure is a simple humanoid shape, but sometimes he can be much more defined, with specific items of recognizable clothing, such as a hat. The dark-man has even made his way into popular culture via TV shows like *Ghost Whisperer* and the iconic horror film franchise *Nightmare on Elm Street*, where Freddy Krueger is the sinister hat-man of your worst nightmares! These pop-culture images then feed back into your psyche, leading to more dark-man dreams, so it can be something of a vicious cycle.

Psychologically, dark-man dreams come from the hidden reaches of the subconscious mind. They symbolize deep and disturbing repressed memories, intrusive, sometimes violent thoughts and your deepest fears personified. If you have a history of being abused, then these dreams can be especially disturbing. In general, though, dark-man dreams are a sign of high anxiety levels that do not abate during sleep. Having such visions indicates that you are feeling overwhelmed, vulnerable and out of control.

In some cases, the shadowy figure could also be a warning against trusting the wrong person, particularly if you have recently met someone who you are not sure about – take this dream as a sign from your higher self that it is safer to keep away from that person. As the name suggests, dark-man dreams are dark harbingers of sinister intention and could indicate that someone is a threat to your safety, or that potential danger is on the cards. Heed the warning, thank the shadowy figure for the heads up, and remember that darkness is dispelled by light, so do things to

increase the light in your life and in your heart. Seek out counselling if you need it, address old issues, heal old wounds, take a holiday to de-stress and surround yourself with a circle of protective light. Once you have acted upon his warning, the dark-man should trouble your sleep no more.

NOCTURNAL FLASHBACKS

Bad dreams can also come about due to illness and mental health issues such as depression, anxiety and most especially Post Traumatic Stress Disorder (PTSD). When someone has been traumatized, often the easiest time for the psyche to deal with traumatic memories, or even just repressed and half-forgotten memories, is during sleep. While amnesia might cloud a person's waking mind, in sleep they are relaxed and therefore better able to receive messages from the subconscious. In this sense, difficult memories can be addressed in the dream state, via nocturnal flashbacks.

Often we imagine flashbacks to be very dramatic experiences, and sometimes they are, but they can also be quite subtle, creeping up on you when you least expect it. This is what nocturnal flashbacks are like, and although they can still *feel* like nightmares depending on what the flashback is about, they are, in fact, memories. Like all flashbacks, they are completely involuntary and you have no control over them – it's not just a case of reminiscing. When you experience a flashback in your sleep, it is all too easy to dismiss it as simply a bad dream or a rough

night, but it is only by paying attention to the visons that they will stop.

Nocturnal flashbacks are a polite way for old fragmented memories to knock on the door of your conscious mind. In short, they want to know if you are ready to handle them in your waking life, so they drop into your dreams to see what you will do with them. Often, these visions then begin to bleed into your waking life more gradually, eventually leading to actual flashbacks during the day, or to a steady drip-feed of additional memories related to the dreams, coming to the surface at random hours of the day, leading you to wonder if you are just daydreaming or losing your wits!

Recurring nocturnal flashbacks can be quite unsettling, especially if they relate to your trauma. A soldier dreaming of being back in the theatre of war, for instance, is basically being re-traumatized on a nightly basis and such dreams will only abate when the initial battle trauma is being actively addressed, usually through an intense period of counselling.

Coping with such dreams can be extremely difficult and means that you are not getting the rest that you need in order to recover. This is because the nocturnal flashbacks effectively mean that you remain stuck in the realms of your trauma, rather than being free to move on with your life. So how do you know if you are having a standard nightmare, or a more intense nocturnal flashback? Well, if you can relate to three or more of the indicators on the next page, you might be experiencing nocturnal flashbacks.

Indicators of Nocturnal Flashbacks

Not all bad dreams are the stuff of nightmares. Some are made from fragmented memories, emotions and physical cues that come from a specific event in your past and they are designed to help you come to terms with old trauma. Common indicators of this include the following and could be a sign that you would benefit from seeking medical help or counselling:

☾ The dream feels more like a memory; it feels real.

☾ You experience the dream in all of your senses through sight, sound, smell, taste and touch.

☾ It feels like you are *living* the dream, rather than dreaming the dream.

☾ The dream is recurring and repetitive.

☾ The dream never changes – it's the same thing over and over.

☾ You cry in your sleep, waking up in tears, on a damp pillow.

☾ You scream in your sleep, waking yourself or others during the night.

☾ You act out the dream in your sleep – walking, crawling, fighting etc.

☾ You feel helpless within the dream or to stop the dream from happening.

☾ You dread going to sleep because you fear the dream is waiting for you.

☾ You feel intense panic, waking up fighting or thrashing around.

☾ You have considered self-medicating with drugs or alcohol to induce a dreamless sleep.

☾ You avoid sleep as much as possible.

☾ You can relate the dream directly to an event or period in your own life.

A Ritual to Come to Terms with Flashbacks

Flashbacks can be very debilitating, but believe it or not, they are actually a sign of healing. When your mind throws up memories in the form of a flashback it is actually processing the events of the past. Often one's instinct is to try to avoid triggering flashbacks as much as possible, however, inviting them in is often a better way of handling them. While this might seem

counterintuitive, when you invite the flashbacks to come to you, you are actually taking charge of how and when the memories come through, by giving them a designated time and space. To do this, find a quiet space where you will not be disturbed, but try to make sure there is someone within calling distance, even if only on the phone. Next light a white candle and say the following words:

A burning flame within my mind
Hidden deep, it keeps me blind
I bring it forth into the light
The past now present, within my sight
Teach me, tell me, show me more
Flashback to a time before
In the present I'm safe and sound
To heal within, the trauma unbound.

Sit or lie in a comfortable position and allow your mind to go where it will. Now that you have given your mind permission to show you the things it wants you to know, you can begin to process the past, one flashback at a time. The flashbacks might come instantly, or you might doze off and experience them in your sleep. They might also come later that day or night. As soon as they have passed, take the time to write them down in your moon journal, pinning the trauma down on the page where it can do you no harm. Repeat this ritual as often as you need to and give your mind permission to speak. Once your subconscious mind feels seen and heard, it is likely that the flashbacks will begin to recede a little.

TWILIGHT DREAMS

Certain dreams are so common that almost everyone will experience them at one time or another. Dreams have long been considered a means of gathering information and insight as we sleep. They are a great way for your higher self to communicate with you, and also for spirit guides, angels, deceased loved ones and other messengers to pass on information. Here are some of the most common dreams and their possible meanings.

Being Chased or Hunted Down

The atmosphere of this dream can be either playful or sinister. If you dream that you are a child again, playing chasing games with friends and siblings, this would indicate that you need to get in touch with your inner child and become more playful in your daily life.

Being chased by a lover in a playful "kiss-chase" kind of way could also indicate that you need to bring a more playful attitude to your relationship, or that you are so fond of the chase you never allow yourself to be truly caught in a committed relationship.

Dreaming that you are being chased by the police or some other figure of authority indicates a guilty conscience. What have you done, or what are you contemplating doing, that goes against your own moral values or the rules of society? Heed the warning of this dream and keep your nose clean, because you're likely to get caught!

Chasing dreams can quickly turn into nightmares, so if you dream that you are being hunted down by someone who means you harm, this would indicate that you feel vulnerable or threatened in some way. It could also mean that someone is a threat to you in real life,

particularly if you have been experiencing dark-man dreams too. Think back over the dream – do you recognize the person hunting you, or is it an unknown assailant? Either way, take extra precautions in your daily life and become more aware of how much information you give away to strangers. Not everyone you meet will be trustworthy, so take care how much trust you place in others.

Crash and Burn

Dreaming that you are in a vehicle that crashes is very common. Cars and planes are the usual modes of transport in these dreams, but it could also be a boat, a train, even an elevator. In these dreams you are in some kind of moving vehicle that suddenly crashes, then bursts into flames or sinks into deep water. This classic dream signifies a feeling of being out of control and suffering the consequences. It can also highlight driver anxiety, or apprehension regarding an upcoming trip or holiday.

If the vehicle bursts into flames upon impact of the crash, this means that you are in the midst of strong, feisty or passionate emotions. This is especially the case if you were the one driving the vehicle, while to watch a vehicle crash and burn in front of you symbolizes that you could be burnt by the emotions of someone else, someone who draws you into a situation against your better judgement – say, for example, a romantic affair. To watch another vehicle crash and burn behind you – say, in the rear view mirror of the car you're driving – indicates that you have had a lucky escape from a situation that would have been harmful or caused you pain.

Crashing into deep water is a sign that not only do you fear a loss of control, but that you are also feeling quite overwhelmed by deep

emotions. If you can escape the vehicle and swim to safety, then all should be well, but if you remain trapped inside, or you find that you cannot swim away for whatever reason, then this is a sign that you need to reassess your life and how much responsibility you take on board. Don't agree to everything you are asked to do and then feel like you've lost control of your life and you're drowning as a result.

Humiliation

Humiliation dreams come in several guises, including dreaming that you are naked in public, that you lose your notes when you're about to

THE HANGED MAN

give a speech, or your voice when you're about to sing or act on stage, or that people are pointing at you and laughing for some reason. In short there is no end to the number of ways in which your dreams can humiliate you! Generally, this kind of dream comes about when you are feeling low in self-esteem or when your confidence has been knocked in some way. Perhaps you have failed an exam, lost your job, or you've just been dumped by your partner, or you've discovered that someone you trusted has deceived you and you feel stupid because of their betrayal. Whatever it may be, this dream is a reflection of that reality. It comes to highlight the humiliation you are feeling and to warn you not to let your confidence plummet any further. Now is the time to start picking yourself back up again.

Flying and Falling

Having dreams that you can fly is a sign of high ambition and future success. This is the case whether you are piloting a plane or flying with a superpower or a magic cape. However, the first indicates that your success will come via external power and support from others, while the second indicates that success will come via your own inner talents and gifts. Flying dreams can be very pleasant, offering the dreamer a chance to look down on their familiar world from a totally different perspective. This perspective can last well beyond the moment you wake up, particularly if you fly away to escape a problem in the dream, as it is likely that you will rise above your troubles in reality too.

To dream that you're falling is a sign that something is about to pull you down to earth with a bump. It could signify a disappointment up ahead, or a failure of some kind. How you fall determines the severity of the disappointment, so if you fall fast and hard, tumbling uncontrollably, then the disappointment will be significant. If, however, you float down more gently, then the disappointment will be a temporary setback. If you dream that someone pushes you from a height, which results in the fall, take this as a sign that someone is trying to tear you down or undermine you in real life. Heed the warning and do what you can to protect your own interests.

Often, flying and falling dreams come about during short periods of astral projection, which is when the astral self floats up and away from the physical body for a short time during sleep. We will be looking at astral projection later in the book, but for now know that when you wake up with a start after dreaming that you're flying or falling, this could be a sign that you have been astral travelling during your sleep.

Wish Fulfilment

There are many different kinds of wish-fulfilment dreams, but they usually involve receiving some kind of extravagant gift, such as a fancy sports car, a race horse or a financial windfall. If you dream that you have won the lottery, get a full house at the bingo hall, or that you are crowned Miss World or something similar, this type of wish-fulfilment dream is a hint as to what you yearn for. Pay attention, because the dream could also contain clues as to how you can make this wish a more realistic goal and something that you can actively work towards achieving.

Sex Idol

Having sexy dreams about someone is another type of wish-fulfilment dream. Usually you dream of someone that you have a crush on but who is beyond your reach in reality, so actors, singers and other famous people. These dreams are great fun to experience and they can put a spring in your step and a smile on your face for the rest of the day. They can also indicate that you might be feeling neglected, or demonstrate a lack of passion, romance and intimacy in your life. Furthermore, these dreams can stay with you for a long time afterwards, making you smile each time you remember them. So next time you wake up after dreaming about your idol, keep your eyes closed, go back to sleep and enjoy it while it lasts!

A POUCH FOR SWEET DREAMS

Magic can be time-consuming, but at some point amid all your moon rituals you will need to sleep. You can't stay up casting spells all night, every night! So here is a little charm bag to ensure that you enjoy sweet dreams when you go to bed. Take a small pouch and place inside it the following crystals: moonstone for dreaming, amethyst for protection, rose quartz for love and obsidian to represent night-time. Next add the following dried herbs: lavender for deep sleep, camomile for calm and mugwort for prophetic visions. Give the pouch a good shake to mix up the contents and place it in the light of the moon for one full lunar month, new moon to new moon. Then place it under your mattress or hang it from a bedpost to work its magic and fill your nocturnal mind with the sweetest dreams. Remember that bedtime can be a magical experience as well as a relaxing one. Sweet dreams!

CHAPTER NINE
LUNAR ANIMALS

Some creatures have long been linked with the moon. Cats, wolves, owls, hares and so on are all thought to have a special connection with the lunar cycle. In magic, witches often call upon the attributes of particular animals for certain spells or needs. So you might call upon the spirit of the cat for greater autonomy for instance, or the wolf for team building. This is known as invoking the spirit of the animal and it is easily done.

INVOKING YOUR LUNAR ANIMAL

You can light candles if you wish, but they are not necessary. Invoking a power animal can be as simple as closing your eyes and asking that animal spirit to guide and protect you. Alternatively, you could wear a charm or bring images and ornaments that represent your chosen power animal into your home. Here are a few of the most well-known lunar totem animals:

Wolves

The image of a lone wolf howling at the moon is an iconic one. Howling is how wolves communicate after all and like most hunter animals, they like to take advantage of the bright night on a full moon. They also howl to find a mate, making their presence known by scenting an area and then howling to draw attention to themselves.

Wolves have no natural predator, which means that technically they are at the top of the food chain – humans require guns and traps to defeat them and so we have usurped their place. Wolves are now a

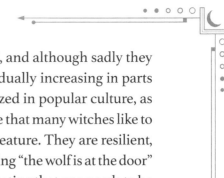

protected species in some parts of the world, and although sadly they are extinct in Britain, their numbers are gradually increasing in parts of Europe. They have been unfairly demonized in popular culture, as have witches, so it should come as no surprise that many witches like to work with the spirit of the wolf as a totem creature. They are resilient, brave, loyal and great survivalists. The old saying "the wolf is at the door" refers to a time of hardship and poverty, indicating that one needs to be strategic in survival, just as a wolf would be. You can call on the wolf for all issues of courage, courting, family, team building, hunting out a good deal or creative survival strategies to get you through the lean times.

Cats

If you have ever tried to keep a cat indoors on the night of the full moon you will know how difficult it is! These little hunters love the moonlight and enjoy their night-time revels. Even house cats tend to act differently during a full moon, often being more playful as they "hunt" their toys. The cat is probably the best-known witch's familiar too, and they do tend to take an interest in magic. They might flip your tarot cards, grab at your pendulum or stare into the flame of a fire or candle.

We can learn a lot from cats. They are such autonomous creatures, often spending their time with neighbours so that no-one ever truly "owns" them. They seem fearless, traversing the neighbourhood at night without a care in the world. They do what they want, when they want and they don't care what anyone else thinks of them. Cats have great confidence and they are not afraid to defend themselves when they have to. As a power animal the spirit of the cat can help you to become more confident, independent, fearless and free-thinking.

Stags and Deer

As creatures of Artemis, stags and deer are inextricably linked with the moon and the hunt. They are prey animals, so they tend to be very highly strung and easily spooked by loud noises and the unexpected. Although their instinct is to herd together, in the autumn the stag rut takes place, so you may come across a lone stag during this time of year, as he is looking for rival stags to fight. They are formidable opponents, yet they can be surprisingly gentle with people, so long as you are quiet and respectful if you are ever fortunate enough to interact with them. While they will never be tame, the stags especially seem to like a certain amount of human contact, coming quite close from curiosity, though the doe deer are much more shy.

The white hart is a pure white stag which is said to hold magical powers. It is a popular icon of medieval art and literature, and a symbol of the hunt. In some depictions the white hart holds the full moon between his antlers, and as the monarch of the glen, he is said to be a royal beast. Magically speaking, he is of course an aspect of the Horned God of witchcraft. As a power animal he can be invoked for issues of self-worth, pride, protection, courage, abundance and prosperity.

Stags have long been linked to royalty and were often hunted by kings and queens and their royal guests at court. They are even given regal names depending on how well developed their antlers are. The points of the antlers are known as tines and the number of tines determines where the stag is in the hierarchy. A stag with 10 tines is known as a "hart of 10", while fewer than 10 tines indicates a "young buck". A "royal stag" has 12 tines, and 14 tines denote an "imperial stag", while 16 tines crown the majestic "monarch of the glen". The more evenly spaced the tines,

the better balanced the stag will be, making him more successful in the rut and therefore more likely to breed. As their antlers are naturally shed each winter, once the rutting season is over, you might find pieces of antler on the forest floor that you can use for altar decorations and craft projects.

Owls

The owl is a bird of two halves. In some cultures, it is said to represent wisdom, magic and alchemical knowledge, while in others it is thought to be a bird of ill omen which brings bad luck. In most places it is considered to be unlucky to see an owl flying during the day. In this respect the owl has a reputation for bringing melancholy on all who see it flying in daylight. As a nocturnal creature the owl is intrinsically linked to the moon, with its round face being reminiscent of the full moon. Some people believe that the owl is an omen of death and there is some truth to this, for it is likely that this association came about because the barn owl in particular will let out a piercing shriek of victory when it has caught its prey. In Scotland the owl is the bird of the Cailleach, the goddess of winter, and it is said that she can shape-shift into one of these birds to go around unnoticed. In most cultures owls are associated with goddesses and the divine feminine.

Magically, owls are linked to the Underworld and the dark half of the year, which is when they are at their most vocal. They are said to be great protectors of magical people, with shamans and druids of the past often wearing an owl feather to denote their standing as a holy man. It is a bird that represents the darker aspects of life: death, winter, night-time, secret knowledge, hidden ways, balance and polarity. As a

power animal the owl can be invoked for issues of academic learning, life lessons, dark nights of the soul, shadow craft, inner wisdom, self-awareness, illness, grief and acceptance of a loss.

Frogs and Toads

Frogs and toads are sometimes thought of as ugly creatures and there is a lot of folklore and superstition to suggest that they may have been severely punished for not being attractive enough! In the past it was common to boil a live toad, or impale it on a branch, after rubbing it onto warts. This was thought to remove the wart. Some frogs and toads are toxic and so they were also "harvested" for their poison. Frogs tended to fare better than toads, as they were thought to bring good luck, while toads were associated with bad luck. Again, this superstition could simply be down to the fact that frogs have a greater level of "pretty privilege", which afforded them some protection!

As creatures of twilight, frogs and toads are most vocal at the rising and setting of the moon, during the hours of dawn and dusk. They are said to be a sign of rain, good harvest and female fertility, which is why kissing a frog was thought to bring a lover, but bear in mind that some frogs carry toxins in their skin so take care if you decide to try this! In some Eastern cultures frogs represent prosperity. In the past they were said to be witches' familiars and witches in disguise. As power animals, frogs and toads can be called upon for issues of transformation, fertility, weather witching, inner beauty, self-acceptance and abundance.

Hares

Like the wolves who howl at the moon and the cats who hunt in its light, the hare is often mesmerized by lunar light, sitting still and looking up in

captivation. To see a moon-gazing hare is said to be extremely fortunate and brings good luck. The hare is a creature of the divine feminine and is linked with fertility, spring and regeneration. In Medieval times people believed that the image of a hare could be seen on the moon, similar to the man in the moon.

Traditionally a hare is thought to be an omen of thunderstorms, and in Britain it is the spirit of the corn, often seen loping through the stubble after the harvest. They have long been considered witches' familiars, and it was said that an accused witch would shape-shift into a hare in order to escape her accusers, bounding away before they had a chance to catch her and put her to the rope or the fire. White hares were said to be the spirits of young women who were jilted or betrayed by their lovers. The white hare spirit would haunt the faithless lover in his dreams until he went mad. White hares are also linked with the season of winter, ghosts and death. As a power animal the hare can be called upon for issues of fertility, renewal, magic, divination, escaping a tormentor and going underground or retreating for some quiet time alone.

Moths

Like the butterfly, the moth is a symbol of regeneration, transformation, renewal and rebirth. However, while the butterfly signifies a positive change, the moth indicates transformation through darkness or difficulty. In short the moth represents a dark night of the soul, where someone is changed at a deep level via adversity or illness. This transformation leads to a stronger character and a rebirth of some kind.

Although some moths fly during the day, particularly on dull days during the darker months of the year, they are generally nocturnal

creatures. A day-flying moth can be distinguished from a butterfly by the way it rests with its wings laid flat and horizontal like a jet, while a butterfly rests with its wings folded vertically. Moths can also be just as colourful as butterflies, but their colours tend to be more muted in tone, to help them blend into the darkness.

They navigate their flight by moonlight, which is why they are naturally drawn to all forms of light. When they circle your lightbulb, they think it is caused by the moon's glow, so they try to reach the deeper darkness on the other side of the light. They will circle the light to the point of exhaustion, so they cause their own demise. In some cultures, the moth symbolizes death and misfortune. For the most part, though, they are simply a winged creature of the night, trying to find their way in the world. As a lunar totem they can be called upon for fresh starts, rebirth, transformation and guidance through a dark night of the soul.

Bats

Bats are considered creatures associated with the Underworld and as such they are linked to the goddess Persephone. They can easily be identified by their erratic flight, which gave rise to their country name of "flitter-mouse". Often you will see them at dusk, just as night begins to fall, particularly during the summer months when there are lots of insects and moths for them to feed on.

Like wolves and toads, bats have been much maligned in folklore and literature, being linked to vampirism, witchcraft, demons and satanic rites. However, they are beautiful, harmless creatures and to watch them flittering across the sky at dusk is a sight well worth seeing. They tend to get dehydrated quite quickly, so if you find one on the ground, offer

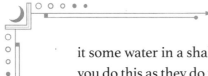

it some water in a shallow bowl or using a pipette. Wear gloves when you do this as they do tend to bite – that part isn't a myth! You can also offer a little dog or cat food to help revive the bat. I have hand-fed bats myself when I worked for a veterinary clinic, and it is such a privilege to help them in this way, and to see the tiny mouth gaping open for more water. They are incredibly sweet! They recover quite quickly and will soon be fit to fly again, once rehydrated.

Bats tend to live in colonies, so where you see one, others won't be that far behind. They prefer to live in tall trees and old buildings such as churches, castle ruins and derelict property. All bats and their roosts are legally protected throughout the UK and Europe, which means that you cannot clear or harm a colony, but must leave them undisturbed. As totems they can be called upon for navigation and finding your own path, intuition, networking and facing fears. There are lots of bat-spotting events held during the summer months, so if this interests you go along and see how many bats you can identify. Alternatively, sit in a garden or meadow as dusk falls and wait for them to appear in the night sky.

Swans

Although swans are more active during the day, they also like to move around at dusk and dawn, which is when they tend to journey between one body of water and another in search of food. If you have ever seen a swan gliding silently across a loch or lake under a full moon, you will be aware of what a ghostly and ethereal presence they can have! Often, this nocturnal gliding is the job of a male swan, patrolling the area around his mate and their nest, especially if they have cygnets to protect.

In Scottish folklore, swans are said to be the reincarnated spirits

of women who died in childbirth. They are associated with the Celtic god Aenghus and his beloved wife, Caer, a fairy-maid, who could both turn into swans and are deities of true love. Swans are associated with purity, fidelity, loyalty, love, strength, honour, the spirit realms and the moon, so they can be called upon for help with all these things. In the UK, mute swans come under the protection of the reigning monarch and all swans are a protected species in general.

These are just a few of the animals that are associated with the moon. There are many more so feel free to do your own research. Working with power animals can be an extremely rewarding practice, as you begin to learn more about your chosen creature and its unique strategies for survival. It is a valuable aspect of traditional magical practice, and as your animal communicates with you through dreams and visions, don't be surprised if your dreams become more vivid after calling on your lunar animal in this way.

CHAPTER TEN
MOON RITUALS

eautiful and mesmeric, powerful and magnetic, the moon deserves to be celebrated in ritual. In witchcraft we call rituals that honour the moon Esbats. Each month witches will work rituals to welcome and honour certain lunar phases, predominantly the new and full moon. We also like to make the most of special moons, such as blue moons and supermoons. Dark moon is considered to be a time of rest, but even this is a way to honour her because the dark moon represents the fallow period before a new season of growth. In resting during the dark moon, witches are honouring that phase by their lack of action. In this chapter we will look at some of the most common forms of Esbat ritual.

DRAWING DOWN THE MOON

Drawing down the moon is a full-moon Esbat and it is a key aspect of Wiccan practice. It is a form of spiritual channelling, wherein the practitioner invokes the lunar goddess energies into themselves for greater power. This power is then redirected into spell craft. This Esbat is about welcoming the power of the full moon into yourself and your life. It could be described as a more active form of moon bathing, where you take the moon's energy into yourself, rather than just basking in her silvery rays. When done correctly a sense of deep calm is experienced, along with a strong pull toward your destiny. This is why people sometimes change their mind about the type of spell they're going to cast after drawing down the moon, because the lunar energies are guiding them

towards a higher path. If this happens to you, just go with it and trust that you are being guided to cast the kind of spell that is for your highest good, one that will have the best outcome for you in the long term.

To draw down the moon you will need to have a clear view of the full moon, so you should ideally work this ritual outdoors. Traditionally you would use an athame, which is a witch's ritual blade, but you can also use your hand. Stand and gaze at the moon until you feel relaxed and centred. Then hold your arms out to the moon, pointing your athame or holding your hands out towards it as if you are going to capture the light. Visualize the moon's energies surging down the blade or through your hands into your body. Take mental note of any particular feelings you experience, such as tingling excitement or a calm sense of purpose. Once you feel that you are full of lunar energies, give thanks and lower your arms. Welcome the full moon with the following words:

I welcome the goddess of full lunar light
I cast in your name this sacred night

You are now ready to cast your chosen spells, using the lunar energies within you as a power boost to your magic. Traditionally women would draw down the moon, while men would draw down the sun during a midday ritual. However, in recent years it has become more common for either sex to draw down the energies of either the moon or the sun.

NEW-MOON ESBAT RITUAL

New-moon Esbats tend to be all about intentionality. At this time, you should decide what it is that you want the lunar energies to bring your way through the course of the coming month. Asking the moon to guide you to your goals is a great way to begin any spell work for goals, ambitions and manifestation.

On the night of the new moon, write down your intentions for the month and what you hope to accomplish. Once you have your goals written down, roll the paper into a scroll, light the end and allow it to burn in a heatproof dish or cauldron, as you say:

New moon of lunar light
Bring me a month of success so bright

Scatter the ashes to the sky and know that you have set your intentions and you have the magic of the moon on your side.

BLUE-MOON ESBAT

The blue moon is the magical moon of manifestation! When there are two full moons in any one calendar month, the second is called the blue moon. It usually only occurs every couple of years, hence the saying *once in a blue moon*. Because it is rare, it is considered to be a most auspicious time for goal-setting, spell-casting and general manifestation. To tap into the sacred power of this moon witches usually cast spells for big ambitions and long-term goals. This is the time to cast for a new house, a change in location, a marriage, a career change and so on. Basically, if

it feels too big for you to achieve on your own and you have no idea how you can bring your dream into reality, then you need to harness the power of a blue moon.

For this ritual you will need an egg and a marker pen. On the night of the blue moon, write your big ambition on the shell of the egg. Reduce the ambition down to one or two key words or a brief sentence if possible, so you might write *I work from home* or *I am a mother.* Be sure to write your goal in the present tense as if it has already happened. Next, take the egg outside into the garden or an earthy space, dig a small hole and bury the egg in the earth, saying:

As the blue moon shines in space and time
It lights the way to this dream of mine

As the egg decomposes, it will slowly release the magic that you have cast and the power of the blue moon will begin to shift things around in your favour. This is a great ritual to cast when you know exactly where you want to be in life, but you don't know how to get there. Allow the blue-moon energies to smooth out the path for you, so that your goal manifests naturally.

BLACK-MOON ESBAT

The black moon occurs when two new moons fall within the same calendar month and again this is indicative of a time of rare moments. When the black moon shines you are being given another shot at something that means a lot to you – a second bite of the cherry, so to speak. The black moon is the time of second chances, double takes, lucky breaks or the return of an opportunity you thought was lost to you. Keep your eyes peeled for signs that second chances are being offered and help them along with this ritual. Take a pinch of blessing seeds, also known as nigella seeds, outside under the light of the black moon. Think of something in your life that you feel you missed out on, something you regret losing. It could be an old flame, a lost career opportunity or an event you missed. Whatever it is, hold this image in your mind as you look up to the sky and the first sliver of moonlight. Now blow the seeds in the direction of the moon and say:

As a black moon edges into view
A second chance returns anew

Learn from your past mistakes. If fear held you back before, accept the second chance with courage. If you let other things hold you back, step forward into this new opportunity with confidence. Take that second bite of the cherry and enjoy it!

SUPERMOON ESBAT

The supermoon is linked to achievement and success, so this Esbat is all about manifesting the rewards of your endeavours. However, you will be expected to work hard for your achievements and nothing is going to be handed to you on a plate. This success could come in any area of your life: love, career, business, family life, adventure etc. – but when you welcome the energies of the supermoon into your life, know that you are about to experience the kind of power surge that only comes from victory. While feeling victorious is a good thing, it can also make people complacent and arrogant. Take care not to let this level of success go to your head and keep your ego in check. To welcome the supermoon, burn three dried bay leaves on a charcoal block and say:

> *I welcome the surge of a supermoon*
> *Hear my request and grant this boon*
> *(state your goal)*

Bay leaves are symbolic of victory, so burning them in offering will ensure that you are victorious in your own endeavours and ambitions. This powerful moon can guide you towards your destiny, so pay attention to the dreams you have during this moon as they may hold key messages from the divine feminine.

PLANETARY INFLUENCES

Alongside the moon, the planets can also have an influence on you and how you view the world. Each planet represents a different aspect of character and you can draw on certain planetary energies to give you a boost in that area. For instance, if you were looking for love, you would work with Venus, lighting candles and incense as offerings to this planetary goddess and invoking her in your rituals. Here are the main planets and how they can be used to build up your character, helping you to become a well-rounded individual who isn't easily fazed by life's little stumbles.

☾ *Sun* – rules your self-image and confidence

☾ *Moon* – rules your emotional intelligence

☾ *Mercury* – rules your intellect and how you communicate with others

☾ *Venus* – rules your ability to give and receive love and open up to others

☾ *Mars* – rules your world view and assertiveness

☾ *Jupiter* – rules your destiny and luck

☾ *Saturn* – rules your self-discipline and sense of personal responsibility

☾ *Uranus* – rules your individuality and self-expression

☾ *Neptune* – rules your imagination and dreams

☾ *Pluto* – rules your self-actualization, motivation and ambition

LITTLE STAR

Wishing on stars is something lots of people have done without even being aware that they are casting a spell! It is something that we teach children to do from a very young age and many cultures throughout history, including the Greeks and Egyptians, believed in its power. So what have you got to lose? Here are some ways that you can start wishing on stars:

☾ Wish on the first star you see each night. This is usually the planet Venus, who shines brightest at dusk and dawn. Gaze at her beauty and make that wish.

☾ Wish on the constellation of your astrological sign. These are the stars that you were born under so you are naturally attuned to their energies.

☾ Wish on a shooting star. These are actually meteor showers which shoot across the night sky. Meteor shower calendars are available online, so you can look up when the next one is due, to give yourself the best chance of seeing these stunning "shooting stars."

THE MOON AS A MUSE

For some people, the moon is an essential collaborator in their creative pursuits. There is something almost sacred about working on a creative project after dark, when the moon rides high in the sky and all the world below is quiet and still. The peace that comes as night falls is vital for writers, artists, musicians, poets, witches and so on. Many people find comfort in their hobbies in the evenings, picking up needlework projects, art therapy or spell craft when the working day is over. Indeed, the hours of darkness might be the only free time they have to indulge in a creative activity.

Artistic magic happens best by moonlight, when the silvery shadows call to mind enchanted portals and ghostly apparitions that feed the imagination and inspire creativity. Many pieces of music, my own "Winter's Nocturne" included, often have nocturnal words in their title, indicating that they were composed to represent the beauty of the night. Beethoven's "Moonlight" Sonata is one example, while the numerous Nocturnes of Chopin are another.

The same is true for some artwork. Consider well-known paintings such as *Night with Her Train of Stars* or *Night,* both by Edward Hughes, or perhaps Vincent van Gogh's *The Starry Night*, or Claude Monet's *A Seascape, Shipping by Moonlight* for instance. With all their moody black and blue tones, it's easy to see the inspirational effect the moon has had on artists down the centuries.

Working throughout the night is a natural process for many creative people, especially those who make a living from their art. Sometimes the daytime is just too bright and busy to get much work done, and so the darkness colludes with us to make artistry and creativity easier. In

this way, the moon becomes a muse to the artist or writer, shining down her light of inspiration.

You can tap into this energy, weaving the moon-glow into your own creative projects by working at night-time. Create a nice routine, where you gather together any materials you need for your project, or go into your creative workspace if you have one, then create a cosy atmosphere in which to work. Grab a hot drink, maybe a blanket to snuggle into as you work, light scented candles or incense and a softly glowing lamp, then set your creativity to work. Repeat this routine every night over the course of a few weeks or months and you will be surprised by how quickly your project progresses. To help you along, cast the following spell to invoke the lunar light into your creative hobby or occupation.

INVOKE LUNAR LIGHT FOR CREATIVITY

Make your creative space all ready for your work and if possible, allow the moonlight to come into the room, or at least leave the blinds open to the night sky. Next, light a tea-light and place it in a holder. Set this within your working area and say these words, or something similar. Repeat the invocation every time you work on your project in the evenings:

> *By lunar light and moon-glow bright*
> *I call the muse of silver light*
> *Creative magic now sealed in starlight*
> *I invoke the muse of the moon this night.*

ASTRAL PROJECTION

Astral projection, also known as astral travel or an out-of-body experience, is the idea that the astral body, or consciousness, can leave the physical body for a short time, giving rise to the dream-like sensation of floating or flying. Some people experience this during times of REM (rapid eye movement) sleep. Spontaneous out-of-body experiences seem to be more likely during times of high stress or illness. It can also be experienced when a person is under anaesthetic during an operation, allowing the sleeping patient to look down on the scene and watch from above.

Although astral projection and out-of-body experiences seem to occur quite naturally as we sleep, some people believe that it can be induced deliberately, or ritualistically, allowing them to go on nocturnal rambles and meet up with other astral travellers along the way. While there is currently no scientific evidence that astral projection actually exists, lots of people claim to have had these types of out-of-body experiences. It is thought that this is where common dreams of flying, falling, floating and levitating originate from.

In certain indigenous cultures, astral travel is actively encouraged and may even be induced with the use of special herbal concoctions. The Native Americans referred to this kind of psychic journey as a vision quest or dream-walking, and it was seen as a valuable tool of insight and self-discovery.

Astral travellers are said to be able to connect more easily with other ethereal beings, such as angels, spirit guides, ghosts, faeries, even aliens. This is because the ethereal self has fewer inhibitions and fears, so it is more open to such experiences. In spirit form, the astral traveller is also thought to have the ability to see glimpses of the past and the future, during psychic visions that are clearly remembered upon waking.

It is commonly believed that the astral self is tethered to the physical body by a silver cord, similar to the umbilical cord. This silver cord ensures that the astral self doesn't stray too far from its physical host. Furthermore, should the physical body be in any danger or detect any sign of threat, then the silver cord instantly pulls the astral self back into the body, meaning that the sleeper experiences a swooping sensation and wakes with a startled jump. This can be quite unnerving, but it is actually a natural reaction known as a hypnic jerk or a sleep start. Here are a few things to bear in mind if you want to try more intentional astral projection:

TIPS FOR ASTRAL PROJECTION

☽ Make sure that you are calm and relaxed. Don't try this technique when you are stressed or poorly.

☽ Sip a cup of valerian tea about half an hour before trying to astral project.

☽ Lie down in a comfortable position.

☽ Spray your pillow with an infusion of lemongrass and vervain essential oils mixed in water, as these herbs are said to aid psychic visions and astral travel.

☽ Ensure the room is at a good temperature, so not too hot or too cold.

☽ Call on your angels and spirit guides to watch over you and protect you.

☽ Put a little moon-dust powder (see page 245) into a pouch and keep this with you for protection as you nod off to sleep.

☽ Think of a place or person you would like to visit as your astral self.

☾ Arrange to "meet" a friend *on the astral* on a particular night.

☾ Hold that image in your mind as you begin to fall asleep.

☾ Tell yourself that you are going on an astral journey to this place or person.

☾ Tell yourself that you will remember your astral adventures when you wake up.

☾ Allow yourself to gently drift off to sleep. Happy travelling!

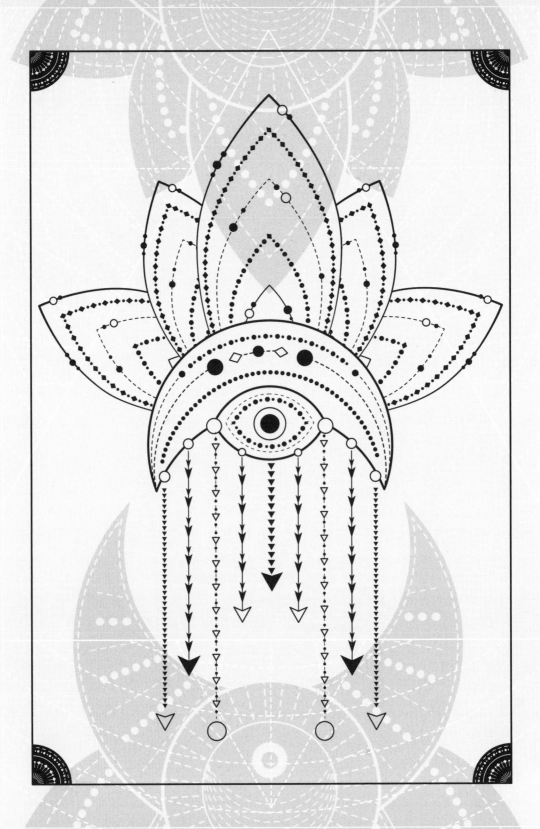

MOON DUST FOR PROTECTION

Moon dust is a popular spell powder, commonly made up of egg shells, salt, ash and sometimes glitter. Eggs shells are frequently used in protection spells because they are designed to protect new life. For this spell you will need a few dried, cleaned-out eggs shells – be sure to remove the entire membrane and allow the egg shells to dry thoroughly. When ready, grind the shells up using a mortar and pestle. Add a teaspoon of sea salt and ashes from your favourite incense and mix it all together. If you wish you can add a little glitter too, but this is entirely optional.

Once mixed up, decant the moon-dust powder into a clean, airtight jar and label it accordingly. To charge the powder with lunar energy, set the jar in the light of the moon, from one full moon to the next full moon. You can then use it as a protection powder by scattering it around outside your home, in your car, in a loved one's shoes or by rolling candles in it for a protection spell.

Moon dust is also very good for wishing spells. Simply take a pinch of it in the palm of your hand, go outside in the evening and make a wish to the night sky as you blow the moon dust away to carry your wish out to the stars.

CHAPTER ELEVEN
MOON FABLES

Fables, legends and folklore are full of enchantment and magic. Often the moon plays a significant role within these stories. Not only are fables the bedrock of storytelling and literature, they are also useful teaching tools, passing down nuggets of wisdom and wise advice to the younger generation. Fables especially tend to hold a kernel of truth or wisdom within the body of the text. In *The Boy Who Cried Wolf,* for instance, the message is clear: don't cry for attention needlessly, otherwise when you actually need help no-one will come to your assistance. In *The Fox and the Wolf*, the cunning fox persuades his cousin the wolf that the reflection of the moon in the lake is actually a large round of cheese. Eager to get to the cheese, the wolf drinks the entire lake and promptly bursts. The twin message of this fable is don't be greedy and don't believe everything you're told!

The most famous fables are, of course, *Aesop's Fables*, which were written by a storyteller in ancient Greece. As a result, Aesop is credited with being the originator of this type of moral tale. His fables usually feature anthropomorphic animals and fantastical creatures from mythology and legend. Rudyard Kipling's *Just So Stories* was published much later, in 1902, yet they follow a similar pattern, using fables to explain various animal behaviours, anatomies and characteristics.

Some fables also include ghostly visitations, supernatural creatures and spirits from another world. These tales were especially popular from Medieval times up to the early 20th century and would be told around the fireplace on cold winter nights. In these more phantasmagorical stories, the original innocent animals from earlier

fables became demonic messengers from hell. Such tales were used by the Church as dire warnings of what would happen if someone strayed outside the fold of Christianity. This type of storytelling was designed to keep people faithful to the Church. It was also used as propaganda during the witch hunts when beloved pets were regarded as witches' familiars and therefore proof of witchcraft. Thus began the demonization of beautiful creatures such as wolves, cats, bats, snakes and rats.

THE FABLED MOON

The moon is often a key feature in many fables and folklore, with faeries, werewolves, vampires, witches and ghosts all said to be more active during the magical phase of the full moon. Certain superstitions came about as a result of these legends. For instance, one superstition states that you should never step inside a circle of toadstools on the night of the full moon or the faeries will steal you away. Another claims that if you wander through the woods during the time of the Hunter's Moon in autumn, the ghostly Wild Hunt might mistake you for a wayward spirit and carry you back to the Underworld, kicking and screaming. And we all know what happens if you get bitten by a wolf on the night of the full moon! In this chapter, then, we are going to explore some of these fabled tales and superstitions.

LYCANTHROPY

In folklore, there are many tales of lycanthropy, which is the legend of people turning into werewolves during the time of the full moon. This transformation usually occurs only after the individual has been bitten by a wolf, though there are also tales of lycanthropy being an inherited condition, passed down from one generation to the next.

In Europe during the Middle Ages, belief in werewolves was so strong that trials for lycanthropy were not uncommon. While women were targeted by the witch hunters and tried for witchcraft, men were sometimes charged with the crime of lycanthropy. In both instances, the accused were usually impoverished individuals with no-one to speak up for them. In lycanthropy trials torture was often used as a means of gaining a confession and the punishment on conviction included being flayed alive and then beheaded. The head would be set upon a spike as a warning to others, while the rest of the body would then be burned at the stake in a public display of victory to demonstrate the collective power of the authorities and the Church over the individual.

Just as with the witch trials, lycanthropy trials were a form of social cleansing and a good way to dispatch any troublesome old tramp, hermit or suspected criminal. During this period of history, the term "wolfshead" was used to denote a criminal, though the crime could be something as innocuous as hunting the king's deer or poaching a rabbit.

In the past, fear of wolves wasn't entirely unfounded because when large packs of wolves roamed the countryside during a harsh winter, they would sometimes feed on untended livestock, pets, possibly even small children, all of which provided the wolves with an easy meal. This added fuel to the fire of superstition and the belief in werewolves, along with their subsequent lycanthropy trials, only began to diminish once the wolves themselves were hunted almost to the point of extinction.

Thankfully the wolf has survived and they are now a protected species, happily roaming free in the mountainous regions of Russia, Eastern Europe, parts of America and the French Alps. A protected pack of wolves can also be found in a conservation wildlife sanctuary in Shropshire in the UK.

Far from being supernatural, in the modern world lycanthropy is now viewed as a psychiatric mental health condition, in which the patient has delusions of being able to turn into a wolf or some other kind of large predator, usually canine, though not always. During these psychotic episodes the patient may exhibit animalistic behaviours such as crawling on all fours, howling and snarling. This mental health condition is extremely rare and it is usually treated with psychiatric medication. That said, the superstition that a full moon can make people crazy and lead to erratic and questionable behaviour is still in circulation today, but there is no scientific evidence as yet to prove this theory.

THE WILD HUNT

Probably one of the spookiest aspects of folklore, The Wild Hunt is well known in various mythologies, including Scottish, Irish, Welsh, Germanic and Norse. As the name suggests, the Wild Hunt is a hunting party, but one that you would not want to saddle up for! It is a spectral Hunt, led by a phantom horseman, with a pack of ghostly hounds running alongside his midnight black mount. Legend states that both horse and hounds have glowing red eyes and foaming mouths, while the horseman is hooded – or headless!

To see or hear the Wild Hunt has long been considered to be a bad omen and although it can be encountered at any time of year, it is more usual for this legend to resurface during the dark autumn and winter months, especially during the time of the Hunter's Moon in October. The Wild Hunt rides in on the billowing clouds of a storm-filled sky. The eerie sound of the hunting horn blows in on the wind, trumpeting through the treetops. The Wild Hunt's purpose is to gather up the souls of the dead and carry them away to the Otherworld.

The Horseman who leads the Hunt is by turns Arawn, Cernunnos, Herne the Hunter, Gwyn ap Nudd, Odin or Woden depending on the region and culture. In Ireland he is associated with Dullachan, a headless horseman who wanders the byways looking for lost souls to take. Again, the Dullachan, or Dark Man, was said to be a harbinger of death. This links back to the dark-man dreams or nightmares of shadowy figures that we looked at earlier, being linked with anxiety, worry, depression, despair and melancholia, so heed this message from your subconscious if you experience such dreams on a regular basis, and seek out help if you need it.

It is safe to say that Washington Irving was probably inspired by the folklore of the Wild Hunt when he wrote *The Legend of Sleepy Hallow* and the Hunt remains a prevalent aspect of spooky folklore. While you are unlikely to see the Hunt in full force, you might experience hints of it – in the shapes of storm clouds or the sound of the autumn wind blowing through the forests and hills. It was said that hiding in a kirk or church would protect one from the Hunt as it rode by, but avoid sheltering under yew trees, for they are portals through which the Huntsman rides and you will put yourself directly in his path!

FAERIE REVELS

The faeries are also said to be more active during the time of the full moon and this is when the Faerie Host is supposed to ride out in the evening. Also known as the Faerie Troop and similar to the Wild Hunt, these trooping faeries ride their fey horses, unicorns and kelpies about the countryside, traversing from one faerie mound or hill to another. Should you get in their way, they will carry you off into Elphame or faerie-land, as their prisoner. The Scottish *Tale of Tam Lin* is perhaps the most well-known fable that recounts this type of abduction.

Signs that the Faerie Host is near include hearing the sound of faerie bells and the jingling of a harness, with no obvious source for the sound. In addition, hearing the blast of a hunting horn is said to herald the arrival of the Faerie Troop,

who are the knights of Elphame. In Celtic folklore these faeries are spilt into two courts, the benevolent Seelie Court and the malevolent Unseelie Court. Crossing paths with either court on a full-moon night was best avoided.

There are also thought to be other fey beings such as sprites, pixies, nixies, elves and brownies out and about during a full moon. These faeries can be helpful towards humans and often grant wishes or help with chores. However, they can be tricksters too, enjoying nothing better than playing pranks on unsuspecting humans. These types of faeries like to gather in faerie rings, which are circles of toadstools, or sometimes stone circles, where they dance, feast and hold faerie revels. Often they will invite humans to join their party, but if you dance with the fey or eat their food, legend says that you will waste away, longing only for faerie food and frolic, while the human world becomes dull and unsatisfying. Christina Rossetti's poem "Goblin Market" was inspired by this aspect of British folklore and states that:

> "We must not look at goblin men,
> We must not buy their fruits:
> Who knows upon what soil they fed
> Their hungry, thirsty roots?"

All in all, it is probably better *not* to step into a faerie ring if you should ever come across one, especially if the moon is full!

WHITE LADIES

Tales of ghostly ladies dressed in flowing, diaphanous white gowns are a common aspect of folklore, told throughout the world. Known as "White Ladies" or "the Woman in White," they are frequently associated with historical figures who died in tragic circumstances and are left haunting the area where they once lived.

These ghostly Women in White are said to appear on nights when the moon is bright or haloed by mist. They have been linked to pagan sabbats such as Litha on the summer solstice, Mabon on the autumnal equinox and Samhain on October 31st. Such pagan apparitions could be linked with the Maiden aspect of the Triple Goddess.

In some legends they are the spirits of women who died in childbirth, or at the hands of violent men, while in others, they are the ghosts of women who committed suicide or whose death was caused by drowning. The latter is more common when the White Lady haunts an area close to a body of water. In more modern renditions of this legend, the White Lady is said to have been a victim of a road traffic accident and she appears to hitchhike or catch a lift from a passing vehicle, only to suddenly disappear again moments later.

Traditionally associated with ancient castles, abbeys and old stately homes, White Ladies tend to wander through the grounds and along roadsides, presumably scaring the local people with their sudden spectral appearance! In some legends she is said to be a harbinger of death or doom, similar to the Celtic Ban Sidhe or banshee. Occasionally she is associated with some kind of curse connected to a particular clan or noble family.

White Ladies are also linked to the Reformation and King Henry VIII's dissolution of the monasteries and abbeys, where they are thought to be nuns who died protecting their home during the violent destruction of the abbey. In some instances, the White Lady is thought to be guarding some kind of treasure or hidden wealth, which ties in with the theme of nuns trying to guard the wealth of their abbey and the Catholic Church.

Whatever her origin may be, the Woman in White has been seen all over the world, yet her preference for appearing to unwary travellers seems to be on dark nights in isolated areas and beneath the silvery glow of the moon, which lends an ethereal charm to her ghostly apparel. So if you happen to be driving along a country road at night, be wary of offering a someone a lift!

GHOST SOLDIERS

Another spectre that has links to the moon is that of the ghost soldier. It should come as no surprise that old battlefields, such as Culloden Moor and Bannockburn in Scotland, or Gettysburg in the United States, might still carry an eerie atmosphere, given the sheer number of men who lost their lives in those locations. However, the dead don't always lie peacefully and there have been sightings of ghostly soldiers still doing battle, centuries after the wars were lost and won. In Gibraltar there is talk of the ghost of a British Army Officer walking his dog through the tunnels that were dug to protect people during air raids in the Second World War. He is said to be an omen of good luck and protection.

Some ghost soldiers date back even further, to the time of the Roman invasion of Britain, with troops of Roman soldiers said to haunt the M6 motorway. It is also thought that the Roman Ninth Legion, which

mysteriously disappeared without a trace, haunts the area around Hadrian's Wall in the UK, forever marching north to Scotland.

In more recent times the legend has developed and now the phantom soldier seems to have taken on a new task – that of guiding serving soldiers through dangerous terrain and enemy territory where improvised explosive devices, or IEDs, are buried underground. This phantom appears out of nowhere wearing a uniform the soldiers recognize and understand to be an ally, then he leads the soldiers to safety, before disappearing. The 1986 song "Camouflage" by Stan Ridgway is a fictional account of this kind of ghost soldier.

It's not just soldiers' spirits that seem to linger, either. In Oxfordshire, an old aircraft hangar that was formerly a part of RAF Grove is said to be haunted by the ghost of an American airman from the Second World War, while a pilot from the First World War is thought to haunt the air station in Montrose, Scotland.

It's no secret that the military take the moon phase into consideration when planning their missions and they use it to their advantage whenever they can. During the Second World War, before the development of GPS, RAF pilots would use the full moon to aid navigation during their night flights. It makes sense, then, that ghostly soldiers and servicemen should appear under a full moon in places where battles have taken place, because for the military the full moon is often a time of activity and great risk. While guidance from a spooky phantom saviour might not be exactly *welcome*, I'm sure the warning is appreciated nonetheless!

CHAPTER TWELVE
MOON
MEDITATIONS

Lunar light is a well-known conduit for visions and intuitive dreams among psychics and seers. Many people find that they experience more vivid dreams around the time of the waxing to full moon, particularly if the moonlight shines into their bedroom. This lunar enhancement of psychic visions can be used during meditation. Guided meditations are great for strengthening your ability to visualize and they are good for gaining insight. Often the higher self will throw up symbols and messages while you are meditating too, which you can interpret after the meditation.

I have designed the guided meditations in this chapter to be gentle and ethereal paths to personal insight and enlightenment. These are mental journeys to magical, imaginary realms. They can be linked together or used interchangeably. Each meditation has its own kind of insight to offer, but this will come from your own intuition, so you need to be open -minded. You can either record them and play back the recording when you want to use the meditation, or you can work with a like-minded partner and have them read it out loud as you meditate, then you do the same for them. The meditations are linked to particular issues.

☾ For ambition and goals use *Once Upon a Winter's Moon.*

☾ For courage in adversity use *Monarch of the Luna Glen.*

☾ For inspiration and destiny use *Midnight Hare.*

☾ For questions about relationships use *Sparkling Swan.*

☾ For finding your soul mate use *Lover's Moon.*

☾ For direction in a crisis use *Soldier's Moon.*

In the following meditations, you will find gods and goddesses, whimsical animals and fey beings, all of which are linked to the moon. I hope that you enjoy working with these extra-special lunar journeys of enchantment.

ONCE UPON A WINTER'S MOON

You find yourself standing upon a sandy beach as darkness falls. The full moon is high over the water as the waves crash in to shore. It is a cold night and winter is just beginning. Your breath mists the air as you begin to walk along the rocky coastline, the grey rocks looming high in the moonlight between land and sea. The sound of the ocean is soothing to you and you enjoy its endless melody as the waves roll in and then recede.

As you walk, you notice a new light on the horizon. At first it is just a glimmer in the blackness of the sky, but soon it grows brighter. It is unlike any light you have ever seen before, glimmering and shimmering over the ocean. As the light develops in shades of blue and green and gold, you realize that you are witnessing the Northern Lights and you stop to admire them. The light swirls around the skyline, going this way and that, with sudden changes in direction as it turns back upon itself. It reminds you of the starling murmurations in autumn, but this movement comes from the ethereal lights in the sky, rather than from a flock of birds. It is mesmerizing and enchanting. The light reflects upon the water, but you cannot tear your eyes away from the Firefox of the night sky, as it dances around the heavens.

Suddenly you hear the gentle hooting of an owl behind you and turning, you see a ghostly shape flying towards you. It is a pure white owl. It lands on one of the rocks and hoots again, almost as if it is greeting you. It has eyes of icy Arctic blue and around its neck is a silver snowflake charm. This is no ordinary owl and you nod your head in respect and say, "Merry meet, Wise One." The owl hoots again, then swiftly takes to the sky once more, swooping down to the beach and perching on another rock, closer to the sea. You follow the bird and say, "As beautiful as you are, Wise One, I know that you are more than you seem. Will you not show yourself to me, that I may get to know you better?" The owl launches itself into the air, where it swiftly transforms into a beautiful woman. She is tall and slender, dressed in a gown of silver and white. Her hair is such a pale shade of blonde, it is almost silver, yet she does not look old. She appears ageless; her icy blue eyes are full of wisdom and knowledge.

"Merry meet, Seeker of the Old Ones. I am Arianrhod, lady of the Silver Wheel and the Stars. I am the one who turns the Wheel of the Year. I weave the tapestry of all life at my sacred silver loom. I turn the tides of the oceans and the tides of your life. I send you the wondrous gifts that change your future – the golden opportunities, the dreams come true and the wishes made manifest, all come from my light."

You thank the goddess for her gifts and thinking back over your life thus far, you tell her which special gifts, talents and opportunities have meant the most to you and why. You tell her what you have done with her gifts and how you have used them to improve your life, and the lives of others. You express your gratitude for all that you have and all that she has given to you over the years.

"You're most welcome, Seeker, for it gives me great pleasure to help you achieve all your dreams. Dreaming is what winter nights were made for! I see all your dreams, I know where your ambitions lie and if you trust me and follow my light, I will guide you to achieve everything that is for your highest good. See those lights on the horizon, the ones that swirl in green and gold, the ones that humans call Firefox and Mirrie Dancers? Those are my lights and they are the portal to my realm. Would you like to see them more closely?"

Arianrhod's icy blue eyes are twinkling in the moonlight as she holds her hand out to you. You nod and take her hand and she leads you further down the beach to the water's edge.

"Will you help me to summon my steeds, Seeker? They aren't far away, but sometimes they can be a little wild and unruly. Will you help me to call them and bring them forth?"

"Yes, I will." Hand in hand with Arianrhod, you both raise your arms high above your heads in invocation, facing out to sea. In a soft voice that sounds like the whispering of gentle waves, Arianrhod begins to chant and you join in with her, saying the words:

"Come Starlight, come Moonlight, come Luna and Glisten
Heed the sea's call, come forth as you listen
White horses fly forward on wave upon wave

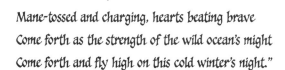

Mane-tossed and charging, hearts beating brave
Come forth as the strength of the wild ocean's might
Come forth and fly high on this cold winter's night."

As soon as the chant is finished, you notice that the sea begins
to surge and bubble, like soup in a cauldron. The waves swell
and plunge, then the white cresting foam takes on the shape of
four wild, white horses, silver hooves beating upon the surface of
the water as they charge out of the sea, tossing their manes and
flicking their tails. Behind them is a snow-white carriage, shaped
like a crescent moon, hung with silver star lanterns on either side
that cast an ethereal glow.

You gaze in wonder at such magic! The four white horses stand
in their silver traces, tossing their heads and snorting, eager to be
off on an adventure. Arianrhod soothes each one with a whisper
and a caress or a pat. Then she turns to you and says, "Come,
Seeker of the Old Ones. Ride with me and see the magic of my
realm." Eagerly, you climb into the crescent-moon carriage and
settle back in your seat. Arianrhod tucks a blanket of white fur
around you both, takes up the reins and with a click of her tongue,
the horses move off into a swift gallop, pulling the carriage behind
them. They gallop along the length of the beach and then with a
mighty leap, they are up in the air and galloping across the sky.

You hang over the side of the lunar carriage and look down
in wonder as the sandy beach disappears below you and the

rocks become specks of darkness, as the horses ascend higher and higher. It is the most exhilarating feeling you have ever experienced. Arianrhod guides the horses straight towards the Northern Lights on the horizon and in mere moments, you are in the thick of them, surrounded by glimmering green and gold as you travel down a long tunnel of vibrant northern light. At the end of the tunnel stands a many-turreted castle, its spires reaching for the stars that surround it. Made from crystal and ice, it shimmers and gleams like a glacier against the backdrop of the midnight-black sky.

Arianrhod pulls up the horses and the carriage stops at the foot of the steps that lead to the castle door. "Welcome to Caer Sidi, the castle of starlight. Come, let me show you around." You leap from the carriage and give a quick pat to the horses, before following Arianrhod and ascending the steps to the castle entrance. The door swings open of its own accord. "It knows me," Arianrhod explains. "Its magic is attuned with mine, just as the magic of your home is attuned with you."

Wandering through the door, you find yourself in a towering great hall. There is a blue-flamed fire burning at one end and in the middle is a table, with two goblets set on a silver tray. Arianrhod picks up the goblets and hands one to you. It is filled with a green liquid that seems to smoke in a vapour that smells vaguely of aniseed and vanilla. "Metheglin, the faerie drink," says Arianrhod. "It is a potion to help visions and inspiration.

Drink, Seeker, for who knows what visions of the future might be waiting for you, just beyond the tipple!"

You sip the metheglin and enjoy the warmth it gives to you, then ask, "What is the purpose of this place, this castle of starlight? What happens here?"

"This is a place of rest, Seeker. Rest for the fallen until they are ready to be reborn into a new life. Rest for the weary until they are able to lift up their spirits once more. It is here in my castle where dreams rest and wait, until the person they are meant for is ready to receive them. Would you like to see my Library of Dreams?"

"Are my dreams kept there?"

"All dreams are kept there safely, watching and waiting, until they are needed. Come, let me show you." She sets down her goblet and walks across the great hall, with you following close behind. There, hidden behind a great tapestry, is a large silver door, carved with magical runes and sigels. Arianrhod opens the door and steps aside, allowing you to enter the room first.

You find yourself in the biggest library you have ever seen. Shelves stretch up higher than the eye can see and each one is filled with scrolls, rather than books. The shelves are sectioned off by subject, but these are not the subjects found in most libraries. Instead you see that sections are labelled in the following way: Dreams, Goals, Ambitions, Talents, Academics, Careers, Wishes, Opportunities, Serendipity, Familiars, Soul Mates and so on. You wander around the shelves, wondering where your own dreams are kept. As if she can read your thoughts, Arianrhod says "They are **all** yours, Seeker. Anything you choose to be and do and achieve, begins right here in this room. This is where your wondrous dreams come true. Look around, find your heart's desire...everything is available to you now, but choose wisely."

You make your way to the section of the library that best fits your own personal dreams and ambition. Arianrhod follows you and says, "Ah yes, I thought you might be drawn here. Choose a destiny-scroll to take with you, Seeker, as my gift to you." You pick out a scroll and tuck it into your belt, thanking the goddess as you do so, for this scroll is the assurance that your dream will soon come true.

"And now we must part ways, Seeker of the Old Ones. Look for me in the Northern Star, make a wish and know that Caer Sidi and I will always be here to help you to make your dreams a reality. Come, and I will show you the way back to your own realm." You follow Arianrhod out onto a balcony, where there is a slide made from starlight. You recognize it as the Milky Way. You turn to thank Arianrhod one last time and she pulls you into a warm hug and says, "Sit for a spell in the starlight, Seeker, and think of me when you do. Now let the Milky Way carry you safe to your own world." You sit on the star-slide and let yourself drop down, down, down, back into your waking life.

MONARCH OF THE LUNA GLEN

You find yourself back in the Luna Glen at dusk. There is a faint light from a waning crescent moon and the landscape has turned to autumn. Muted shades of amber and gold will soon be lost to nightfall, but right now you see the brown of faded heather on the hillsides, the russet and gold of turning leaves. The glen is swathed in autumn mist that swirls around, hiding the summits of the mountains. The fog of your breath mingles in with the mist around you.

The air is damp and you set off walking towards the tree line up ahead to seek shelter. Leaves crunch under foot and you kick the autumnal carpet as you go, just as you did as a child. It feels pleasant to tramp through the leaf-fall. It reminds you of all your autumns past, as the year sheds the weight of former glory and prepares for the next stage of growth. You realize that is what you are doing too – shedding old woes and former triumphs, and preparing for new challenges and the personal growth that they bring.

The evening is still, but for the sound of your own footsteps... and then, someone else's. Someone is walking behind you, at a distance, but coming closer. You stop in your tracks and look over your shoulder to see who it is, but no-one is there, nor can you still hear their footsteps. You turn back and continue on your journey. Once again, the footsteps resume behind you, closer this time. Listening carefully, you realize that the sound is different from the one your feet make as you walk. Rather than a gentle trudge, this is a clop, clop, clop, clop, in a steady rhythm, just behind you. Someone, or something, is following in your footsteps. It moves when you move, it stops when you stop.

You look round again, but still you can't see anyone, yet you can feel a presence and it isn't human. You wonder who is following you and in the spirit of courage, you decide to stand your ground. Turning, you stand in the depths of the glen and call out to your mysterious companion, "I know you're there! I can hear you. Who are you?" There is no reply, so you say, "I am a Seeker of the Old Ones, I mean you no harm. Will you show yourself to me?"

There is silence in the misty glen and no-one answers your call. You wait for a few moments, taking in your surroundings as night descends upon the glen and the waning moon offers little light. Still nothing, only silence and the gentle sound of your own breathing. You continue on your walk as the shadows deepen, trudging through the leaves as quietly as you can, listening out for any sound, but all remains still and you imagine your silent companion has found a different path.

All of a sudden you hear a loud bellow and the sound of thunder. No, not thunder...hooves! A wild, rampaging stag comes charging out of the tree line just ahead and gallops full pelt towards you. You stand your ground. You are not afraid, just wonderstruck. He is beautiful! He has a full rack of antlers and you estimate that he carries at least 16 tines, possibly more, bearing them proudly upon his head. He gazes at you for a moment, then throws up his chin and bellows again, before lowering his antlers to the ground, using them to toss the autumn leaves around. When next he lifts his head, he has russet leaves, old thistles and bits of grass hanging from his antlers. He looks like a Yuletide tree and you giggle at the sight of such a bold, majestic creature looking so ridiculous!

The stag clip-clops towards you on cloven hooves. As he comes closer, you notice that his fur is pure white, his antlers silver-grey and he gleams, even in the shadows of the night. He is a white hart! You watch in awe as this most magical and enchanted of stags walks towards you, sure-footed in the leaf-fall upon his dainty hooves. He stands a short way in front of you, bellows again and tosses his antlers. He is waiting for something.

Then it dawns upon you that this magical creature with sixteen tines is the Monarch of the Luna Glen and you are a guest in his realm. You remember your manners and give him a respectful nod, saying, "Merry meet, White Hart! I am honoured that you should come to welcome me to your beautiful glen." The stag bows his head in acknowledgement and comes closer. Once more, he lowers his head to the ground, but this time he is trying to catch your scent, sniffing up the length of you, from your feet, right up to the hair on your head. Seemingly satisfied that you are harmless, he nuzzles your hair, then blows gently on your face in greeting.

When the stag pushes his nose into your hand, you take this to be an invitation to pet him, so you stroke the velvety fur of his face and muzzle. You are close enough to gaze into the liquid brown of his eyes, to breathe in the earthy scent of him – like mud and moss, berries and leaves. He smells of the autumnal landscape that is his home. You gently scratch the middle of his forehead and he pushes towards you, playfully nuzzling your hair in reciprocation of your grooming fingers.

Next the stag nods towards the floor and somehow, you just know that he is asking you to kneel down. Placing all your trust in him, you kneel before the majestic beast and hold your breath in wonder as he gently rests his chin on your right shoulder, then your left, followed by your right shoulder again. The Monarch of the Luna Glen has just knighted you! You are now a peer of his Moonlit Realm.

As you remain kneeling, the stag places his muzzle to your heart and gently breathes his strength and courage into you. You feel his vibrant magic coursing through your veins and you know that whatever life sends your way, from now on, you will always have the courage of the stag with which to face it. You reach up and put your arms around the white hart's neck, hugging him in gratitude for the gift he has just given to you. To your great surprise, the stag kneels also and once again, you have a deep knowledge that he is inviting you to climb onto his back. Carefully, you mount the stag and settle yourself down in the curve of his spine, holding onto the thick white fur of his ruff. In a smooth motion, the stag raises himself up onto his forelegs, then his hind legs push you up high off the ground and he trots off back into the Moonlit Forest. He carries you easily, as if he is used to bearing your weight. You smile in glee at the feeling of riding through the woods on the back of a wild stag, his antlers spread out before you, his hooves churning up the forest floor. When he breaks into a canter you clutch tightly onto his ruff, digging your fingers in even deeper in an effort to keep your seat. Gaining speed, he lifts his chin so that his antlers flatten against his sides, resting by your legs, as the tree trunks speed by in a blur.

This is pure freedom! The ground slips by beneath you and the branches catch at your clothes. The dancing silver hooves beat out the rhythm of the forest and you are exhilarated by it. This is like flying! You laugh in joy at the wonder and speed of it all, as the stag gallops along full tilt, carrying you through the Moonlit Forest. He is nimble and swift, dodging tree roots and overhanging branches with perfect ease. He is showing you what he can do, what it means to be a stag and run free with the deer herd. He is proving that you will always be safe in his care; no danger could possibly catch up with you when he spirits you away like this. He is allowing you to experience the kind of strength and speed that you could never achieve on your own two feet. He snorts as he gallops, his breath and yours mingling in the night air, becoming one together as you ride swiftly through the shadows and ribbons of mist.

Weaving and turning, dipping and ducking, the stag carries you further into the deepest part of the forest, nipping in and out of the halls of trees as if they are not even there. The two of you make a ghostly sight, the white hart and his astral rider, flashing by in a streak of sliver and white, his hooves drumming on the forest paths and deer tracks, your gasps of delight the only sounds hanging on the night air.

The trees begin to thin out and you notice that the stag has carried you all the way through the Moonlit Forest. Now you are back in the open air of the glen, but still he does not stop. Instead he gathers his strength and begins to dash up the hillside opposite the forest, snorting as he goes. Instinctively you lean forward, to help him up the gradient. You can feel his hind legs powering the two of you up the steep slope of the glen. He is tireless! Up and up and up, until you reach the highest point of the mountain range and very crest of the glen.

Then the white hart gathers his quarters beneath him and makes a mighty leap into the unknown, into the void on the other side of the mountain and you feel yourself catapulted forward... into the nothingness of air. The magic white hart vaporizes underneath you, turning into silver mist, and you are left floating gently down, down, down, back into your waking self.

MIDNIGHT HARE

You arrive in the Moonlit Forest at the stroke of midnight. The witching hour is here and anything can happen! You feel a sense of excitement and anticipation as you begin to walk along the forest path. The moon is almost full tonight and the silver light filters through the tree canopy and dances on the carpet of bluebells around you. You breathe in their heady fragrance and watch as they nod their heads in the night breeze as you pass. It is almost as if they are bowing down to you in greeting. Then you notice something that makes you stop in your tracks.

Up ahead, in the middle of the path sits a hare, her grey-brown fur silvered in the moonlight, her face turned up towards the sky. She sits in perfect stillness, gazing lovingly up at the moon. It seems as though she has been hypnotized. She is mesmerized by the moon. You are mesmerized by her. Her long ears are folded along the curve of her back and her nose twitches slightly as she sniffs the night air. You wonder if the moon has a scent that only she can smell. All of a sudden her trance is broken and she becomes aware of your presence. In a flash she is off, dashing through the forest, her bob-tail flashing white in the moonlight.

You take off after her, struggling to keep up because she's so fast! Her hind legs power her forward in great leaps and bounds as she makes her way to a clearing in the forest. You chase on, stumbling over tree roots as you go, but you know that you will never catch her. In the middle of the woodland grove is a large ring of red and white toadstools. You recognize the faerie ring just as the hare leaps into it and promptly disappears! Without hesitation you leap into the faerie ring after her, experiencing a swooping sensation and darkness, before thumping to the ground in a heap.

Looking around, you witness the hare transforming into a pretty faerie. She is small and dainty, with rosebud lips and large brown eyes. Her ginger hair is curly and wild, falling in spirals to her chin. The skirt of her dress is made from white petals and she wears the trumpet of a white flower on her head as a hat. You blink in fascination, for you've come to realize that you are in the presence of a shape-shifting faerie, not a real hare at all. "Merry meet, Fey One. I am a Seeker of the Old Ones and I apologize if I startled you in the woods."

"You didn't startle me," the faerie reassures you. "Welcome to Elphame, Seeker of the Old Ones. This is the land of the faeries. I am Moonflower. Look for me in the moonbeams bright, feel my magic only at midnight. I have been waiting for you, so that I could show you something. Come with me."

The faerie flies ahead, fluttering on silver gossamer wings. You follow in her wake, walking through a forest similar to the one in your own world, but here the bluebells tinkle like real bells in the breeze, and you can see lots of tiny eyes peering at you from the foliage. Moonflower leads you towards an old well, set in the middle of a crossroads in the forest. The well bears a sign that says *Well of Inspiration – Drink and Know Thy Destiny!* There is a golden chain, from which hangs a matching ladle.

"Will you drink from the golden cup, Seeker, and discover what kind of inspired action will lead you to your destiny?" Moonflower asks, perching herself neatly on the wall of the well.

"I will!" you say, as you turn the handle of the well. The golden ladle begins its descent into the darkness. It takes a long time until you hear a faint splash, then you start to draw the ladle back up again. When it reaches the top of the well, you reach forward and pull the ladle toward you. It is full to the brim with a pale, frothy amber liquid. "Drink, Seeker, and allow yourself to be inspired in the nights and dreams to come," says Moonflower encouragingly. You take a sip from the ladle and taste a myriad of flavours at once – spearmint, vanilla, sugared almond, wild cherry and more, all rolled into one. It's delicious and you eagerly drink the whole ladleful. All at once you hear music that you hadn't noticed before.

"What is that music? Where does it come from?" you ask.

"Oh that's just the goblin market. They can be a bit rowdy sometimes. Come, I'll show you." Moonflower flies up into the air and you hurry to keep up with her, until you come to a vibrant market town. Looking around you see all manner of fey folk from goblins and elves to pixies, faeries and brownies. Some are calling out their wares from behind colourful stalls, some seem to be casting magic spells, others are browsing or bartering. You make your way through the crowded market place, entranced and enchanted with the charm of it all.

At the far end of the market you notice a brightly coloured Maypole, bathed in moonlight, with ribbons twining and fluttering as a group of faeries dance around it. As you get closer, Moonflower grabs your hand and drags you towards the pole. "Dance with me Seeker! Let your worries go and join in the Faerie Revels!" She places a coloured ribbon in your hand and before you know it you are part of the dance, circling round the Midnight Maypole, weaving your ribbon as you dance in and out with your fey companions. The circle dance grows faster and you run to keep up, laughing and enjoying yourself. You feel alive and vibrant, youthful and carefree. This joyful fey magic is good for you. The dancers circle round and round, faster and faster and faster, taking you with them, until suddenly your ribbon snaps off the Midnight Maypole and you spin wildly away from the dance, away from the market and out of Elphame, floating down, down, down, back into your waking self.

SPARKLING SWAN

You are standing on the edge of a loch. The full moon is shining down, her silvery beams reflecting on the water in dancing light. It is a misty evening and the mist rolls over the loch in smoky clouds. You can smell the pine of the surrounding trees and see your breath in the chilly night air. As you gaze over the water, a beautiful swan glides out of the mist. In the moonlight he looks ethereal and ghostly, a phantom bird gliding upon his enchanted loch. His progress across the water seems effortless, but you know that he is working hard beneath the surface, his feet paddling away, powering him forward, steering him in the direction he wants to go.

He is regal and poised, holding his power quietly inside himself. For all the swan's beauty, they are not flashy birds and you appreciate the quiet confidence that the swan exudes. You wish that you could be more like him. You want to drink in his grace and charm, his strength and power. To you, it seems that he is a Swan Prince, quietly patrolling his watery home, graceful, even as he watches for predators and those who would trespass upon his magical realm.

As the swan moves smoothly across the moonlit water, you track his progress from the shore, walking along the water's edge to keep up with him. Then, you come upon a silver boat that has been intricately carved, so that the prow is a swan's head and the sides of the boat have been made to look like folded wings. It bobs gently upon the surface of the loch, moored with a golden cord. Laid within it are a pair of golden oars and round about the prow is written the words *Swan Blessed*.

Eagerly you untie the boat, push it further into the loch and jump in. Picking up the golden oars you make your way steadily towards the centre of the loch, where the mystical Swan Prince seems to await you. The water feels heavy as you row, but you push the oars against its resistance and power the swan boat out into the deeper water. Once in the middle of the loch you rest on the oars and look around for the Swan Prince saying, "Merry meet, Swan Prince. I am a Seeker of the Old Ones. Will you come closer?"

With a ruffle of feathers and a shake of his tail he glides forward, then lowers his head and half opens his wings in a courtly bow, which you return with a nod of the head. As the swan gets closer to the boat, he swims directly over the oar and you begin to pull it in, but notice that he is playfully enjoying the movement of the water which the oar creates. You move the oar in a large circle, under the paddling feet of the swan, then out and over his head. He shakes the water droplets from his head and waits for the oar to come underneath him once more. It is almost as if he is skipping in the water, using the oar as a child would use a skipping rope. His sense of fun and frolic makes you giggle and you continue this game for a while.

With a trumpeting sound, the swan tucks his head under his wing and begins to nibble at his plumage. You imagine that he is simply grooming himself, until moments later he reappears with one of his purest, whitest feathers in his beak. Stretching out his long, slender neck, he gently drops the feather in your lap. It is a gift from the Swan Prince and you tuck it into your pocket with gratitude. "Thank you Swan Prince. I will keep it forever, close to my heart and every time I see it, I will remember our meeting and think fondly of you, here on the loch."

Another trumpeting call sounds in the distance and with a glance over your shoulder, you see a second swan gliding out of the mist. The Swan Prince has a mate! She meanders across the water and you wish her a good evening as soon as she comes close. Then, the Swan Prince dips his head into the boat and tugs out the golden cord, used for mooring. He holds it in his beak, and his mate does likewise. Both swans then begin to pull the boat across the water, into the mist. You stow away the oars and enjoy the ride, thinking how pleasant it is to be pulled along by two kindly, magnificent birds such as these.

As the mist envelops you, it is difficult to see where the swans are taking you, but you have a deep trust that they will guard, guide and protect you. For now, you lie back in the boat, gazing up at the moon and thanking your lucky stars that such magical creatures seem to know that they can trust you too. You drift off into a slumber, as the boat rocks you to sleep.

A little while later, the swans start to make low trumpeting sounds and you awaken, feeling rested and refreshed. Sitting up, you notice that they have pulled the boat towards a small island, hidden in the middle of the misty loch. Then to your great surprise, as the swans' feet touch land, they transform into people! The Swan Prince becomes a tall, muscular warrior in Celtic dress, while his mate becomes a beautiful woman, dressed in a golden gown of rich velvet. You stare in wonder and they smile at you mischievously.

"Don't be alarmed," says the tall man, formerly the Swan Prince. "I am Aenghus, Lord of Love, and this is my wife, Caer. You are most welcome here on Cygnet Isle, Seeker. Anytime you yearn for the peace of my loch, simply blow three times upon the feather from my wing and you will be back in my realm. But now, let us feast!" Aenghus leads the way further onto the island, where there is a round table set with many dishes of fine food. The table and matching chairs are made from twigs and the whole thing has the appearance of an elaborate nest. You feast with the Celtic god and goddess of love and purity, enjoying their company and protection. If you have questions regarding your own love life, now is the time to ask them and allow their guidance to come to you.

Once the feast is over, Aenghus rises to his feet, raises his goblet and says, "A toast to love and to all that are open to it! It is a difficult journey for most of us at times, a tragic one for others and a lonely path until it be found, but it is the meaning of life. To find a soul to mate for life with, heart to heart and spirit to spirit...that is a journey worth embarking upon. To love!" You raise your goblet and repeat the toast, smiling with enthusiasm. Gently, you stroke the feather in your pocket – Aenghus's promise that he will always be there to love, guide and protect you, and you know that he will guide you to your true soul mate if you are brave enough to follow his lead.

"I have a gift for you too, Seeker," says Caer shyly. "Here is a Pearl of Wisdom that will guide you to make the right choice in a mate, and in other dilemmas too. As my husband says, the path is never easy, but this Pearl will help you to find your true soul mate and Anam Cara – your soul friend. It will help you to make brave and bold decisions." With these words, Caer drops a creamy, iridescent pearl into your hand. You hug her in thanks and place the pearl carefully in your pocket beside the swan feather.

"And now, Seeker of the Old Ones, it is time for you to return to your own realm. Know that you can come back here whenever you need to, and in the meantime, look for me in the swans on the water and in every white feather that you find, for that is my way of letting you know that I am watching over you. Always. Now, climb upon my back and I will take you home."

You clamber onto the piggy-back that Aenghus offers and as soon as he feels your weight, he begins to run along the shore of the island, turning swiftly back into the mighty Swan Prince. With a leap, he ascends into the air, his mighty wings outstretched, with you on his back and you look down to see Caer, his wife, waving to you and smiling as you leave. You dig your fingers into the soft white feathers of Aengus's slender neck and blow a kiss to the full moon as you pass her by. Then suddenly, the Swan Prince is swooping in a thrilling dive through the sky and you feel yourself dropping down, down, down, back into your waking self.

LOVER'S MOON

You find yourself standing on a sandy beach, silvered in the light of the full moon, which sails high in the sky, illuminating the ocean below. You are feeling lonely tonight, wondering where your life partner is and what you might do to bring them closer to you. Lost in thought you walk through the shallows of the water, allowing the warm waves of a summer ocean to wash over your feet. It is grounding and relaxing and you begin to feel more content.

You pick up a stick and write your name in the sand, along with the dearest wish of your heart. This wish will remain in place until the tide carries it away to the universe, and at some point it will be returned to you in reality. You feel the truth of this deep down, but sometimes it can be hard to trust that all good things are coming to you, especially when it comes to romance. You've had your fair share of ups and downs, and it can be frustrating at times. Still, you know that there is someone you are meant to be with. All you need is a sign that they are coming to you, that you won't be apart forever and that you will find one another.

You sit on the beach and gaze out over the water. The sound of the waves gently lapping into shore soothes your troubled spirits and you relax. You notice that the moonlight creates a shimmering path across the water, from the full moon on the

horizon, all the way into shore. You wish that you could walk on water to see where the path leads, but as you stare at the Moon Path, you notice that there is a figure standing on the horizon, silhouetted by the moon.

The figure begins to walk towards you, following the Moon Path of light across the ocean and suddenly you know that this is the soul of the person you are meant to be with. You stand to greet them and wait for them to make their way to you. They walk steadily along the path, not rushing, but coming to you at their own pace. This steady progress reminds you that all things unfold in their own time, not yours. Patience is required, especially in matters of love and the merging of twin souls, but here is a lover who would cross oceans to be with you.

As the figure walks in to shore, you notice they are still shadowy and indistinct. You cannot see their features; there is nothing to help you recognize them in life. They are simply a soul that is meant to connect with your soul. You hold your hands open in welcome and they step onto the sand and take your hands in theirs, then they pull you into an embrace. You feel your heart flood with a myriad of emotions – safety, compassion, trust, acceptance, loyalty, desire, support, attraction, comfort, affection, admiration, respect, humour, protection, consideration, care – this is what love is meant to feel like. This is how you will know that you are in the presence of a soul mate or soul friend.

"I've waited so long for you," you say. "I'm still waiting for you."

"I am coming. Don't give up on us. We are meant to be, and I will find you, I promise."

"But when? I've waited and waited, and you're still not here!"

"I am here now, my love, and I am forever in your heart, as you are in mine. Dance with me, let us enjoy this time and space, while we can." And there, beneath the light of the full moon, with the sound of the waves coming into shore, you waltz with your soul mate, feeling truly happy, and deeply loved, for perhaps the first time. You feel their energy mingling with yours, their soul twinning with yours, the recognition that this is something extra special, a love like no other you have experienced before.

The dance swirls you both around and around, as you move to the combined beat of your two hearts. You are smiling and laughing with your lover, enjoying being in their company, feeling safe and protected. Feeling loved and loving, an equal exchange of affection and respect. When you stop dancing, you walk along the beach, hand in hand. There is no need for words between you, because you know how each other feels and the silence is one of contentment and trust. Suddenly, your lover bends to the ground, picks up a pebble and gives it to you. It is a perfect heart shape. "Hold onto this until I find you, my love. This is my promise to you, that I will do whatever it takes to reach you."

You take the pebble from your lover and say, "And I will do whatever it takes to accept you and trust you when you come into my life."

"And so our soul-pledge is made. Look for me in the light of the moon on the ocean, see me in the love hearts that fill your world and know that I am coming to you."

"But how will I recognize you?" you ask, fearful again that love might pass you by and leave you lonely forevermore.

"You will know me by the way that you feel in your heart. Look for the one with… and know that it is me." Your lover gives you a clear sign to watch out for, some way to recognize them in the real world. This is just between the two of you, a secret sign that indicates when you are in the presence of your Anam Cara or soul mate.

Your lover then picks up a stick and when you look down, you see your own name written in the sand, and your lover writes their initial beneath it, then encircles both names in a love heart.

"Fear not. Our love is sealed in the sands of time, and now, my love, it is time for me to go and for you to return to your own realm. Know that if ever you feel lonely, I am right here on the Moon Path and you can meet me here, whenever you want, until I find you." Gently your lover takes your face in their hands and kisses you sweetly on the lips, in a promise of things to come. Then they turn and walk back out onto the Moon Path, walking across the ocean. You know that you must let them go, in order

for them to find you in reality. You hold tightly to the pebble and the promise it represents, as the sand beneath your feet starts to give way and you are gently sinking down, down, down, back into your waking self.

SOLDIER'S MOON

You find yourself back in the Moonlit Forest and the light of the full moon filters through the trees. You are stumbling along, pushing through dense undergrowth and feeling branches swiping at your face, catching at your hair. You feel exhausted, as if you are in the midst of something that is bigger than you are able to cope with. You stand for a moment catching your breath and you realize that you are hopelessly lost and alone. You don't know which way to turn or which path to take. Despite the moon, everything feels dark and foreboding. All you see is darkness and black shadows in the night.

In a panic you stumble blindly ahead, the twigs cracking beneath your feet. Worry dogs at your heels. However hard you try you cannot outrun it. You wonder when you lost control, when things began to go wrong for you and an image comes to mind, suggesting that, deep down, you already know the exact point at which you took a wrong turn, or the circumstances that brought difficulty into your life. A turn that has led you here, to this moment in time, when you are struggling to see the forest for the trees. Try as you might you can't seem to fight your way ahead. You feel like giving up, giving in and just letting the forest take you, allowing the ivy and brambles to bury you in their strangling grip.

Then someone grabs you from behind. You struggle but to no avail, for the arms that encircle you are strong. Your captor

whispers in your ear, "Shhhh! It's okay. I'm on your side. I'm going to let you go, but don't run – this place is a mine field. Understand?" You nod your head and the arms that hold you loosen, allowing you to shake yourself free, and you turn to face your captor.

Before you stands a soldier wearing full camouflage gear, bits of leaves and brambles sticking out of his helmet, his face painted in shades of green and grey and black, so that he blends into the shadows of the forest. On his jacket he wears a badge that you instantly recognize as an ally. He is telling the truth. He is on your side and you can trust him with your life.

For the first time in a long time, you relax and breathe a sigh of relief. You no longer feel alone. Now you have backup. Strong backup that can help you through the current situation. You see that the soldier is watching you, assessing you, to determine how much fight remains in you. "Okay?" he asks in a whisper. You nod and he replies, "Right then, let's crack on. Put your hand on my shoulder, or tuck it into my belt and follow me." You do as he says and follow in his footsteps. He seems to know exactly where to go and in moments, he has led you deeper into the undergrowth and motioned to you to crouch down, where you are both hidden from view. For the first time, he smiles at you and says, "Sometimes, Seeker, you just have to wait it out for a bit. Give yourself a moment to think and breathe. Just breathe." You take a couple of deep breaths and feel your nerves begin to steady. His eyes remain fixed on you. He's completely unafraid of his environment. Then he asks you a question – "What's your mission? What brings you here?" – and you find yourself telling him about the issues that you are facing right now.

"I just don't know which way to turn," you admit, "I don't know how to get through this. It all feels like it's too much."

"Don't worry, I'll get you to the next checkpoint and you'll receive your next detail of command there. I know it's tricky, but you can do this. I know it's scary, but you're strong and brave. You might feel alone, but you have backup, you just have to look for it in the right places. All soldiers feel alone from time to time, but we're part of a bigger team and we work together to complete whatever mission we've been given and to achieve the best results. That's what you're doing right now. You're working on the mission and exploring options."

"But I just don't know what to do! How do I get out of this situation? What's the point of it all?" you ask him, to which he replies, "You don't need to see the bigger picture, Seeker. You don't need to know how your whole life plays out. All you need to see is where the next safe step is. All you need to do is take one safe step after another, one foot in front of the other, and that's enough to get you across any mine field. Are you ready for the next step?" You nod your head and the soldier says, "Right then let's navigate this mine field. Stay behind me and I'll guide you safely through to the other side."

As before, you follow in the soldier's footsteps, your fingers tucked into his belt, trusting him to lead you in the right direction and get you to a safe place. His presence is very reassuring. It takes time, and progress is slow, but this gives you a chance to mentally work through the issue at hand. You tread carefully, taking the soldier's advice and putting one foot in front of the other. In time you exit the woods and come to a hidden sentry point at the edge of an open field. Another soldier is waiting for you there and your solider introduces you and says, "The Seeker has come for their next detail of command."

"Ah yes," says the sentry soldier, "I have it here." He hands you an envelope, which you open and take out the sheet of paper it contains. On the paper is written a clear instruction of what you need to do next, or where you need to look for support. You put the note into your pocket. This is your next command from the universe and the guidance that you seek.

Suddenly you hear the sound of an aircraft and looking up you see a helicopter approaching through the night sky. "Taxi's here!" laughs your solider. "Right, Seeker, this is where I leave you. Take your command and follow it to the letter. When you need further instructions, you know where to find me. Good luck with your mission and stay safe!" He grasps your forearm in a soldier's handshake and then he turns and makes his way back across the mine field and into the forest. The sentry soldier leads you out toward the helicopter and helps you into a backpack of some kind. You climb into the helicopter and thank the pilot for taking you to safety. "Don't thank me yet, you might not like the way home!" he laughs. Puzzled, you settle back in your seat and watch the Moonlit Forest disappear below you. An airman sits beside you, but he is busy looking over the terrain. All of a sudden, he turns to you and says, "Get up, it's time." You get up and without another word, he pushes you right out of the helicopter midair! The backpack jerks behind you and with relief you realize it's a parachute that opens automatically. The canopy opens up above you and you float gently down, down, down, back into your waking self.

XVIII

THE MOON

CONCLUSION
SHOOT FOR THE MOON!

From astrology and Wicca to shooting stars, meditation and magical planets, I hope that this book of lunar enchantment has served to whet your appetite for making magic with the heavenly bodies. Moon magic and ritual is a fascinating topic and now that you have read this introduction to it, you might want to delve deeper and read more about it, so take a look at the Further Reading section for some book recommendations.

Remember that we are all made of the same atoms as make up the universe, so essentially, we are all made from stardust! The planets might be a long way away, but we are certainly connected to them, both spiritually and naturally, by their influence on the earth and their place within our solar system. Understanding the moon can help you to understand yourself a little better, from your moods to your dreams, so I hope that you will take some time to try out some of the rituals and techniques within the pages of this book. Use the lunar energies to propel your life forward and allow her silvery beams to carry you *through adversity to the stars*. The power is always there, so tap into it. Wish on stars, align with the planets, work with your higher self in these guided meditations and above all, always shoot for the moon! *Per ardua ad astra*. Farewell until our next merry meeting...

Blessed be,

Marie Bruce

FURTHER READING

Books by the same author:

Wicca
Celtic Spells
Moon Magic book and card deck
Book of Spells
Green Witchcraft
Wicca for Self-Transformation
The Wiccan Guide to Self-Care
Celtic Magic book and card deck
Glamour Magic

BOOKS ABOUT THE MOON

DRIESEN, Tamara (2020). *Luna,* UK, Penguin Random House

GALENORN, Yasmine (2000). *Embracing the Moon,* USA, Llewellyn Publications

GALLAGHER, Kirsty (2020). *Lunar Living,* UK, Yellow Kite Books

GREENLEAF, Cerridwen (2017). *Moon Spell Magic,* USA, Mango Publishing

KANE, Aurora (2020). *Moon Magic,* USA, Quarto Publishing Group

McCOY, Edain (1998). *Lady of the Night,* USA, Llewellyn Publications

MOOREY, Teresa (2003). *Silver Moon,* UK, Ebury Press, Random House

ACKNOWLEDGMENTS

There are many influences that go into writing any book and this one is no exception. I am extremely grateful to my mother for her suggestion that I include some Native American folklore in this book and for her constant support of my dreams. Thanks Mum, love you to the moon and back!

I am also indebted to my friend and fellow creative, Jamie Llewellyn, for his beautiful album, *Moon Lore*, which provided a fitting soundtrack for this project and kept my mind in the right space when I was busy working on the book. You can find Llewellyn's art and music at www.relaxationman.com

I owe a million thanks to the team at Arcturus, for their generous support of my ideas and the wonderful writing opportunities they keep sending my way. I love writing for you guys and I look forward to working on all the new projects we have coming up! Signing with Arcturus was one of the best things I ever did. Thank you for giving me a space where my creativity can grow.

Then of course there are my soldier friends, especially the one I nicknamed Kermit, who also inspired parts of this book. I am grateful to all my friends in the military, both veterans and those currently serving in the British Army, the RAF and The Red Arrows. You know who you are! This book would not be what it is without your inspirational, motivational influence in my life. Some of you were *still* deployed as I wrote this book, but I want you to know that you are never out of my thoughts, or my protection. I am so proud to call you my friends and to surround you all with as much protection magic as I can conjure. There is room on my broom for all of you!

Of course, not all influences are human – some are places, some are animals. The main creative influence throughout my work has always been Scotland, in this case Strathpeffer and Oban. Parts of this book, the meditations in particular, were greatly inspired by my own experiences in these two Highlands towns. In Strathpeffer, I witnessed the Northern Lights and I was indeed stalked and "knighted" by a majestic Red Deer stag, who I then befriended (aka bribed with carrots!) and stepped out with every night. Also, in both Strathpeffer and Oban, on two separate occasions, a male swan proudly presented me with one of his beautiful feathers! I keep one of these feathers tucked into my planner, as a reminder that we can learn a lot from animals. The Strathpeffer swan also enjoyed skipping with oars! I always knew that such magical encounters would make it into my books one day, so I am delighted that I was able to write them into the meditations in *Moon Magic*.

Last but not least, I would like to thank all the readers who have stuck with me since the beginning, since way back in the late 1990s. Thank you to those who have supported my work and followed my career from publisher to publisher, from books to magazines to music and back to books again! I *see* your loyalty and I appreciate each and every one of you. We may never meet, but I know you're there and I wish you all good things. Blessed be.

Love to you all, Marie xxx